CW00547962

SUSANNA WESLEY

and the Puritan Tradition in Methodism

JOHN A. NEWTON

SUSANNA WESLEY

and the Puritan Tradition in Methodism

Second Edition

LONDON

EPWORTH PRESS

All rights reserved. No part of this publication may be reproduced,
stored in a retrieval system, or transmitted,
in any form or by any means, electronic, mechanical,
photocopying or otherwise, without the prior permission of
the publisher, Epworth Press.

Copyright © John A. Newton 2002

British Library Cataloguing in Publication data

A catalogue record for this book is available
from the British Library

0 7162 05629

First published in 1968 by Epworth Press
This new edition published in 2002
4 John Wesley Road
Werrington
Peterborough
PE4 7ZP

Printed in Great Britain by
Biddles Ltd, www.biddles.co.uk

To
RACHEL

CONTENTS

PREFACE

THIS study had its origin in reading undertaken for the Dr George Eayrs Essay in Methodist History, whose subject for the year 1959–1960 was *Susanna Wesley*. I am most grateful to the Rev. N. Allen Birtwhistle (General Secretary of the Methodist Ministerial Training Department), and the late Dr Alan Kay (the then Connexional Editor), for their encouragement of the suggestion that the essay might be expanded into a much fuller treatment of the subject. Dr Kay's successor, the Rev. Gordon S. Wakefield, has continued his interest in the project, and laid me under obligation by his friendship and scholarly advice.

Other friends to whom I am indebted for the stimulus of their informed criticism are: the Rev. Sidney O. Dixon of Mullion, Cornwall, the late Rev. W. L. Doughty, Dr Geoffrey Nuttall of New College, London, and the Rev. Henry D. Rack of Hartley Victoria College, Manchester. In addition, I should like to express my thanks for facilities afforded me to consult books and manuscripts, to Dr Frank Cumbers, the Book Steward; the Rev. W. F. Flemington, former Principal of Wesley House, Cambridge; the Rev. A. Raymond George, Principal of Wesley College, when at Headingley, Leeds; Mr Edward Milligan, Librarian of the Friends' Historical Society; Dr Geoffrey Nuttall, as Librarian of New College, London; and Dr Roger Thomas, Librarian of Dr Williams' Library. What I owe to my wife, who has not only refused to regard Susanna as a rival, but has consistently encouraged me in this task, the dedication can do no more than hint.

JOHN A. NEWTON

Wesley College, Bristol

PREFACE TO THE SECOND EDITION

SINCE this study of Susanna Wesley was first published in 1968, there have been considerable changes in the life of the Methodist Church, and marked advances in Wesley Studies. Not least among these changes has been the enhanced role of women in the ministry of the Church. At the 1974 British Methodist Conference, the first women presbyters were ordained, and they and their successors have since made a notable contribution to the life of the Church.

Again, the last thirty-four years have seen a great increase in women's scholarly writings—in theology, biblical studies, ethics, philosophy of religion, church history, and spirituality. We may be confident that Susanna Wesley would have rejoiced to see both these developments. She herself was unusually well-read in theology, and had gifts as pastor, educator, and spiritual guide which were to have a formative influence on all her children, and notably on her two distinguished sons, John and Charles. In many ways, she is an icon of women's ministry.

The revised and expanded bibliography in the present work attests the growth in the amount of published work—both popular and scholarly—that has recently been devoted to Susanna. Students of her life and work are particularly indebted to an American scholar, Professor Charles Wallace Jr., who in 1997 published *Susanna Wesley: The Complete Writings* (Oxford University Press). This invaluable volume makes available much material previously accessible only in manuscript form, and brings together for the first time all Susanna's letters, journals, educational, catechetical and controversial writings.

Professor Wallace rightly observes, in his Preface, that, 'Given the keen interest in recovering women's voices in the history of both church and society, the time is ripe for a careful presentation of the work of Susanna Wesley'. I would also strongly endorse his contention that Susanna 'deserves to be regarded not just as the mother of the founders of Methodism but also as a fascinating figure in her own right, a woman enmeshed in and yet pushing against many of the patriarchal constraints of early eighteenth-century church and society'.

My hope is that the republication of this biography of Susanna may serve to encourage the growing interest in an outstanding Christian woman, who began life as a Puritan Nonconformist, became an Anglican, and finally joined 'The People called Methodists'.

JOHN A. NEWTON

Bristol, November 2001

INTRODUCTION

THE dictum which urges that 'Mothers are the makers of spirit', can cite an impressive range of evidence in its favour. Certainly the most superficial knowledge of the character and career of John Wesley can hardly overlook the enormous influence of his mother on his whole personal development. Mrs Elsie Harrison's study of Wesley deliberately allows the accent to fall on the crucial human relationship of his life, when it styles him *Son to Susanna*.[1] It is indeed arguable that this relationship is the vital clue, not merely to his private life, as Mrs Harrison's title suggests, but to much of his public life—they were never far apart in Wesley—and to his whole personal make-up too.

If Susanna's influence was so vital for her son's development, then it becomes imperative to try to understand her own character and beliefs, and the environment, both personal and intellectual, which helped to shape them. When we turn to the sources available for such study, we are confronted by the surprising fact that there has been no attempt at a full-scale biographical study of Susanna. Certainly there is no life of her extant which is at all commensurate with the central importance she holds both in the life of John Wesley and in the development of Methodism. The present study is not a full-length portrait of Susanna, but attempts to set her

[1] G. Elsie Harrison, *Son to Susanna: the private life of John Wesley* (1937).

life and thought within the context of the Puritan tradition in which she was bred, and to assess the importance of her Puritanism for the upbringing of her family and for the development of Methodism.

For such a study of Susanna there is no lack of materials. Adam Clarke's *Memoirs of the Wesley Family*[1] contains a valuable selection of Susanna's letters, prayers, and theological writings. More of her letters are printed in G. J. Stevenson's *Memorials of the Wesley Family*.[2] Many of her meditations and prayers have survived, partly in her own manuscript notebooks at Wesley College, Bristol, and partly in printed sources.[3] A brief selection of this devotional material has been edited by the Rev. W. L. Doughty in *The Prayers of Susanna Wesley* (1956). In addition, one of the most important of Susanna's theological treatises, setting out a reasoned basis for the Christian Faith, was published by the Rev. G. Stringer Rowe in 1898, under the title, *Mrs Wesley's Conference with her Daughter*.[4]

Yet although materials for Susanna's life were to hand, it was not until 1864 that the first published life appeared.[5] It was the work of a Wesleyan Methodist minister, the Rev. John Kirk, who lamented in his Preface that though there had been numerous brief sketches of Susanna's character, yet 'up to this hour, no volume worthy to be called a memorial of her has issued from the press'. He hoped 'to supply, in some small degree, this remarkable deficiency'. Despite the rapid sale of his first edition, it can only be said that Kirk's turgid and pietistic account fully justified the modest claims he made for it. There followed, in 1876, a volume in the *Eminent Women Series*, entitled *Susanna Wesley*,

---

[1] First edition, 1823; for the purposes of this study, the second edition, revised and enlarged to two volumes (1836), has been used.

[2] Published London, no date, but with Preface dated 1876.

[3] Notably in Adam Clarke, op. cit.; J. Whitehead, *Life of Wesley* (1793); H. Moore, *Life of John Wesley* (1824); and *The Wesley Banner* for 1852.

[4] Publications of the Wesley Historical Society, No. 3.

[5] J. Kirk, *The Mother of the Wesleys* (1864).

and written by one of her distant relatives, Eliza Clarke. This life is clear and readable, and shows real shrewdness of judgement in assessing character. It is vitiated, however, by a pronounced tendency to undervalue the religious basis of Susanna's life and thought. In her preface, Eliza Clarke admits that Susanna was 'nothing if not religious', but at the same time appears to count it a virtue in her own biography that it 'differs from previous ones in not being written from a sectarian nor even from an eminently religious point of view'. What this approach means in practice may be seen in her omission of a long and interesting section of a letter from Susanna to her son Samuel, then at Westminster School, with the complacent remark, 'Much of this letter has been omitted on account of its being exclusively a theological dissertation.'[1] It is symptomatic of Eliza Clarke's approach that, while she devotes a whole chapter to 'The Supernatural Noises' (the Epworth 'ghost' or poltergeist), she refers hardly at all to Susanna's theological writings, her prayers or meditations. When Susanna's letters take on a theological tone, as they often do, Eliza Clarke's tendency is to excise the offending paragraphs and subsume them under a row of asterisks. She gives herself away in her Preface, where she clearly implies that the religious element in Susanna's life is of only secondary interest: 'More of general interest about Mrs Wesley ought to have been preserved; but, unfortunately, she and her family have been regarded solely in connection with Methodism. She was nothing if not religious; but [*sic!*] she was a lady of ancient lineage, a woman of intellect, a keen politician, and, had her ordinary correspondence been preserved, it would have given us an insight into the life of the period which would have been full of deep and world-wide interest.'[2] By 'ordinary

---

[1] Eliza Clarke, *Susanna Wesley*, p. 98. For the full text of Susanna's letter, see Clarke, *Wesley Family*, II, 146–50.
[2] Eliza Clarke, *Susanna Wesley*, p. vi.

correspondence' is apparently meant 'non-religious' or 'non-theological'. The possibility that the letters which have come down to us from Susanna's pen, full as they frequently are of theological meat, might represent her 'ordinary correspondence', or an important part of it, never seems to have entered Eliza Clarke's mind. She would clearly prefer an expurgated edition of Susanna's writings, 'without theology', and does her best to provide it for her Victorian public. But Susanna without theology is rather like *The Fathers without Theology*, to quote an egregious modern title,—or like *Hamlet* without the Prince of Denmark. If Kirk errs on the side of religiosity in his presentation, Eliza Clarke distorts the picture of Susanna by trying to water down the strain of religion which is central to her whole life and character.

The third and most recent life of Susanna is Miss Mabel R. Brailsford's *Susanna Wesley, the Mother of Methodism*, published by the Epworth Press in 1938. In many ways, despite its brevity, Miss Brailsford's is quite the best life of the three. Herself a Quaker, but the daughter of a Methodist minister, Edward John Brailsford (1841–1921), she has an understanding sympathy for the religious dynamic of Susanna's personality. She writes lucidly and with a discerning humanity. She is not content, for instance, to dismiss Susanna's method of educating her children as harsh and inhuman, as a superficial reading of it might suggest. 'Her views on the training of children,' she writes, 'may sound somewhat arid and harsh, for the atmosphere of mother-love cannot be captured and held in a syllabus. Here again her system can be judged only by its results, and there was not one of the young Wesleys but left her schoolroom endued with the twin passions for learning and for righteousness.'[1]

All three of the extant lives of Susanna deal quite cursorily with her early years in the London home of her father, Dr Samuel Annesley, one of the most distinguished of

[1] M. R. Brailsford, *Susanna Wesley*, p. 63.

Puritan ministers. Yet her Puritan home and her close relationship with her father were of decisive importance for Susanna. None of the previous lives really brings out the key significance of her ancestral Puritanism for her whole later development. It is hinted at and touched upon, but never documented or explored in depth. This omission may be seen as typical of a more general neglect of the Puritan strand in the Methodist tradition. One may fully concede the many-sided nature of the Methodist movement, and the diversity of influences—Catholic, Anglican, Pietist and Moravian—which helped to shape it. Yet, as I have written elsewhere, 'there is another strand in Methodism which, while not ignored, has often been underestimated or minimized—the English Puritan tradition in which Wesley's parents were reared. It is true that both Samuel and Susanna Wesley left the Dissent of their birth, but one cannot jump out of one's skin by a change of denomination, and the evidence suggests that Susanna at least never lost her Puritanism even after she became a loyal Anglican.'[1] These words might serve as a text for the present study, for Susanna Wesley incarnated many of the values of Puritanism, bred them in her children, and so transmitted them to Methodism, where they formed part of the rich amalgam which was the result of John Wesley's creative work for English Christianity.

It is not suggested, of course, that one can understand any complex event *merely* by reference to its antecedents; nor is it denied that tracing everything back to Adam can be a tedious and unprofitable procedure. Yet if it is agreed that Susanna Wesley exercised a decisive influence on her son John, by character, relationship, and teaching, then it surely becomes essential to investigate the influences, personal and

[1] J. A. Newton, *Methodism and the Puritans*, (Friends of Dr Williams's Library, 1964), p. 2. In this study I have tried briefly to indicate the debt of Methodism to the Puritans, under the heads of doctrine, liturgy, pastoralia, and ethics.

intellectual, which formed her spirit. Chapters One and Two describe Susanna's Puritan home and background, and draw freely on the writings of her father and his fellow-ministers. Chapter Three examines the marital relationship of Susanna and Samuel Wesley, and utilizes new material which has come to light as recently as 1953. Chapter Four is devoted to Susanna's training of her children,—practical, moral, and religious,—and to the theological treatises she wrote for their instruction. Chapter Five leans heavily on her own writings, especially her prayers and meditations, and tries to assess how decisively Puritanism shaped her devotion and theology. Chapter Six looks at Susanna's reactions to the Methodist Revival, and her influence upon its course. Chapter Seven seeks to assess how far Susanna's Puritanism affected the doctrine and ethos of Wesley's Methodism. Chapter Eight describes her death, and forms a brief epilogue to the whole study.

Despite some obvious differences, there are clear resemblances between the Puritanism of the seventeenth century and the Methodism of the eighteenth. Both stand in a dialectical relation to the Church of England, originating within it, and yet standing over against it. Both make their fundamental appeal to Scripture, and look to reason and experience to corroborate its deliverances. Both embody a conception of the Christian life in terms of disciplined living ('method' is a keyword for each of them), moral rigorism, and Christianity in earnest. Both stand for warm popular piety and lay religion, genuinely of and for the people. Both are intensely concerned for evangelical mission and pastoral care, and are ready to adapt and supplement the system of the Church in obedience to these primary needs. Both, finally and supremely, are concerned with the sovereignty of grace, and are eager to translate into human terms an understanding of the Christian life as 'faith working by love'. Can we, however, posit more than a family likeness between these two traditions? Can we discern continuity within a given stream of Christian life? It is the argument of this study that we can, and that the central figure in the transmission of the Puritan tradition to the life of Methodism is she who found it no inconsistency to be a Puritan, an Anglican, and a Methodist, and who embodies all three types of churchmanship: Susanna Wesley.

CHAPTER ONE

'The Saint Paul of the Nonconformists'

There is not a greater service done to the devil's
kingdom than the silencing of faithful ministers, and
the putting them under a bushel that are the lights of
the world.   *Matthew Henry*

ON the twentieth of January 1669, there was born
to the well-known Nonconformist divine, Dr Samuel
Annesley, the last of his twenty-five children, a girl named
Susanna. She was the child of his age, for Dr Annesley was
a man of fifty when Susanna was born to his second wife at
their house in Spital Yard, off Bishopsgate Street.[1] She was
the child of his age in a deeper sense too, for to the end of her
days she remained a daughter of the seventeenth century,
which had seen the triumph and eclipse of Puritanism. It was
in this century that her Christian name first became widely
current in England, and though she soon left the Dissent in

---

[1] The house still stands, and, under the name of Annesley House, serves as
headquarters of the Women's Fellowship of the Methodist Church. See
Frederick C. Gill, *In the Steps of John Wesley*, (1962), p. 43f.

19

which she was reared for the Church of England, Susanna emerged, like her name, with the stamp of that Puritan century clear upon her.[1]

Susanna's mother, whose Christian name is unknown, was the daughter of John White, a Puritan lawyer who sat in the Long Parliament as member for Southwark, and distinguished himself as Chairman of the Committee for Religion. He published in 1643 an account of the first hundred clergymen whom the Parliament had deprived of their livings for immorality or neglect of duty. The title of the book, *The First Century of Scandalous Malignant Priests*, earned him his nickname of 'Century White'.[2] Of Susanna's father, Samuel Annesley (1620–96), whose life spans almost as much of the seventeenth century as his grandson John Wesley's does the eighteenth, much more is known. He was born at Kenilworth in Warwickshire, the son of John Annesley, whose father had been granted an Irish peerage by Charles I. John's elder brother, Arthur, succeeded to his father's titles, and was later admitted to the English peerage as the first Earl of Anglesey.[3]

Edmund Calamy, writing about Dr Annesley some thirty years after his death, records that, 'He was descended of a Good Family; and I am inform'd his Paternal Estate was considerable. His Father died when he was four Years old; and his religious Mother took great care of his Education. He was strongly inclin'd to the Ministry from his Infancy; and was not discourag'd in it by an affecting Dream he had while he was a Child: Which was, that he was a Minister, and sent for by the Bishop of London, and to be burnt for a Martyr.'[4] At the age of fifteen, Samuel Annesley went up to Queen's College, Oxford, and proceeded B.A. in 1639, on the

---

[1] For the name Susanna, cf. *The Oxford Dictionary of English Christian Names*, Ed. E. G. Withycombe, 2nd ed. (1950), p. 26of.

[2] s.v. John White. See *Dictionary of National Biography* (afterwards *D.N.B.*)

[3] *D.N.B.* s.v. Samuel Annesley; Clarke, *Wesley Family*, II, 362.

[4] Edmund Calamy, *A Continuation of the Account of the Ministers, Lecturers, Masters and Fellows of Colleges, and Schoolmasters, who were Ejected and Silenced after the Restoration in 1660, by or before the Act of Uniformity.* 2 vols. (1727), I, 65.

eve of the Civil War. He then disappears from sight during the first few confused years of the conflict, until, on the twentieth of December 1642, we find his name listed among the Puritan lecturers or preachers sanctioned by the Long Parliament: 'Samuel Anneley [*sic*] Lecturer of Chatham (Kent).'[1] Yet, though already preaching, he was not ordained—as a Presbyterian minister—until two years later. His ordination certificate, signed by seven senior ministers, relates that he has been chosen to serve as a chaplain aboard the warship *Globe*, which formed part of the fleet under the command of the Earl of Warwick, the Parliament's Lord High Admiral.[2]

His naval service was not continuous, however, for by 1645 he had become the Rector of Cliffe, Kent, a wealthy living worth some three hundred pounds a year.[3] At Cliffe Annesley replaced Dr Griffith Higgs, a cleric who was not acceptable to the Parliament.[4] His own allegiance to the parliamentary cause gained him other distinctions, besides his living and his naval chaplaincy. At the instance of the Earl of Warwick, who 'had other Chaplains that were Doctors' and 'was willing that Mr Annesley should be a Doctor too',[5] the University of Oxford did the patriotic thing and made the young chaplain a Doctor of Civil Laws in 1648. In this same year he was chosen to preach to the House of Commons at a solemn monthly fast-day, on July the twenty-sixth. The members assembled in St Margaret's, Westminster, and heard the young minister announce his text from the Book of Job, chapter 27, verses 5 and 6: 'God forbid that I should justify you: till I die I will not remove

---

[1] *Commons Journals*, II, 897, as cited in W. A. Shaw, *The English Church 1640–1660*, II, 304.

[2] See Calamy, *Continuation*, I, 66f.

[3] See *Proceedings of the Wesley Historical Society*, II, 53. For the valuation of the living, see John Walker, *Sufferings of the Clergy of the Church of England* (1714), Part II, 267.

[4] See Walker, op. cit., Pt. II, 39.

[5] Calamy, *Continuation*, I, 67.

my integrity from me. My righteousness I hold fast, and will not let it go: my heart shall not reproach me so long as I live.'

The Commons must have wondered what was coming next, after this announcement of unshakeable integrity. They were soon to find that this young man of twenty-eight, for all the preferments he had received from Parliament, was no time-server. He proceeded fairly to trounce the members, by way of recalling them to their duty to maintain strict integrity of faith and practice. Far from being overawed by the occasion, he claimed it as the privilege of ministers to 'propose sifting Interrogatories'—in other words, to ask searching questions—and proceeded to do so in no uncertain terms. His first 'interrogatory' set the tone for all the rest: 'And first, let me ask you, what you are in matters of Religion, and the power of godliness? For present forget your greatness, and give account of your goodness (if you have it); do not some of you cause the Enemies of God to blaspheam, & the very name of Reformation to be a by-word among those that hate it?'[1] The members of the House can hardly have sat easily under his probing series of questions: 'What ends had you in seeking or accepting publick employments? . . . What have you done in point of Justice? . . . Have you let slip seasons of Reformation?'—a question clearly expecting the answer yes. He ended by urging them to humiliation, repentance, justice, integrity, resolution, and in a final word 'To the People' somewhat ironically warns them not to disparage their Magistrates.

In this sermon of Annesley's there is no smooth flattery of a distinguished congregation. It is typically direct, search-ing, Puritan preaching, though perhaps its sharp edge is made sharper by the fiery idealism of a young man and the

---

[1] *A Sermon preached to the Honourable House of Commons, July 26, 1648. At Margarets Westminster, being The Solemn monethly-Fast day. By Samuel Annesley, L.L.D., Preacher of the Gospel at Cliffe in Kent.* In the spirit of self-mortification, the Commons ordered the sermon to be printed.

tense state of the war.[1] By August he was at sea again, and prepared the sermon for the press, 'aboard the *George* riding off Goree in Holland', where the Parliament's fleet had sailed in pursuit of the ships which had gone over to Prince Charles.[2] His sea journal ended in November, and by mid-winter he appears to have returned to his pastoral charge at Cliffe. He had been strongly critical of Charles I in his sermon to the Commons, but he drew the line at regicide and by his own account 'publicly detested the horrid murder' of the King. In 1651, when Cromwell defeated Charles (II) at Worcester, Annesley 'refused to send a horse against his Majesty . . . and despatched a servant at night from a distance of forty miles to secure the church keys, in order that no schismatical ministers might hold a thanksgiving service in his church in celebration of Cromwell's victory'. His outspoken criticism of Cromwell ('the arrantest hypocrite that ever the Church of Christ was pestered with'),[3] apparently lost him his living of Cliffe, for he spoke of himself later as 'necessitated to quit a parsonage worth between two and three hundred pounds per annum. and get into the least parish in London, without any other title besides the choice of the people'.[4]

The 'least parish in London' was St John the Evangelist, Friday Street, where he began work in 1652.[5] Despite his opposition to the Cromwellian regime, he was appointed in 1657 to preach 'a lecture on the Lord's Day afternoon in St Paul's Cathedral',[6] and received one hundred and twenty

[1] Part of the Parliament's fleet had revolted. See note under 27 July 1648 in Carlyle, *Oliver Cromwell's Letters and Speeches*, 3rd ed. (1888), p. 278.

[2] Calamy, *Continuation*, I, 67. Annesley kept a journal of this spell at sea, and for notes of some of his sermons preached on shipboard, see *Historical MSS Commission, 12th Report*, Appendix, Pt. IX, 177.

[3] For Baxter's similar charges against Cromwell, see *The Autobiography of Richard Baxter*, ed. J. M. Lloyd Thomas, (n.d., Preface 1925), p. 69f.

[4] J. Stoughton, *History of Religion in England (1640–1700)*, (6 vols., 1881), ii, 42–3.

[5] Clarke, *Wesley Family*, I, 366.

[6] *Calendar of State Papers Domestic 1657–8*, p. 52.

pounds a year for doing so. The next year he was authorized by Richard Cromwell, the Lord Protector's son, as Vicar of the great parish of St Giles, Cripplegate, where he remained until the Restoration brought a drastic change in the religious settlement.

Dr Annesley's ministry at St Giles ended with a bang rather than a whimper, for in September 1661 there was held in his church a special series of 'morning exercises', or daily preaching services, at which leading Puritan ministers took turns to officiate. The 'Exercise' had begun as a prayer meeting in the dark and confused days of the Civil War, when,

Most of the citizens in London having some relation or friend in the army of the Earl of Essex, so many bills were sent up to the pulpit every Lord's day for their preservation, that the ministers had not time to notice them in prayer, or even to read them. It was therefore agreed to set apart an hour at seven o'clock every morning, half of it to be spent in prayer for the welfare of the public, as well as particular cases, and the other in exhortations to the people. Mr Case began it in his church in Milk-street, from whence it was removed to the other distant churches in rotation, a month at each. A number of the most eminent ministers conducted this service, in turn; and it was attended by great crowds of people. After the heat of the war was over, it became what was called a Casuistical Lecture, and continued till the Restoration. The sermons were published in six volumes quarto.[1]

On the fourteenth of November 1661, Dr Annesley wrote his editorial preface to the first of these six volumes, which bore the title, *The Morning-Exercise at Cripplegate: or, Several Cases of Conscience Practically Resolved, by sundry Ministers, September 1661.* It was to be one of his last acts as Vicar of St Giles, for the year 1662 confronted 'sundry Ministers', including Annesley, with a very searching and personal 'Case

---

[1] D. Neal, *History of the Puritans*, ed. J. Toulmin (5 vols., 1796), I, 797. 'Mr Case' was Thomas Case, author of *The Morning Exercise Methodized* (1660). Dr Annesley edited the first four volumes of the published sermons—in 1661, 1674, 1682, and 1690.

of Conscience', and one which had to be most 'Practically Resolved'.

To conform or not to conform, that was the question. With the restoration of the monarchy came the restoration of the Established Church, of the Prayer Book, and of episcopacy. For the moderate Puritan, the dilemma was an agonizing one. Should he make the declaration required by the Act of Uniformity, which involved a complete endorsement of every jot and tittle of the doctrine and liturgy of the Prayer Book, a step which, for men like Annesley in Presbyterian orders, would mean re-ordination at the hands of a bishop? Or was he to heed the pastoral needs of his people and the economic circumstances of his family, take the Oath, swallow his scruples, and hope for a measure of reform and toleration in the Church as time went on? Annesley, in company with many of the finest of the Puritan ministers, men of the stamp of Richard Baxter, Daniel Williams, and John Wesley's great-grandfather Bartholomew Westley, chose to foresake his benefice rather than violate his conscience, and so ended his term as Vicar of St Giles.[1]

1662 was to prove the great watershed, the beginning of the time of troubles for Nonconformity, and the source of that long tension between 'Church' and 'Chapel', which, if it has diversified, has also bedevilled, English religious history. Though for many years moderates on both sides made brave attempts at comprehension and reunion, the breach grew steadily wider, and 1662 proved to be a real turning point in the religious life of the nation. Puritanism—the attempt to purify, transform, revolutionize the Church from within—now gave way to Nonconformity, separately organized, with its own ministry, training colleges, congregations and meeting-houses, standing over against the

[1] According to Annesley's son-in-law, John Dunton, the living of St Giles was worth £700 a year. See *The Life and Errors of John Dunton*, ed. J. Nichols (2 vols., 1818), I, 367f.

parish church and the hierarchy of the Establishment. Despite a myriad personal contacts across the divide, and a leavening of Christian charity which survived all the persecution and bitterness, English religion could never be the same again.

Yet though Annesley had surrendered his living, he had not given up his ministry. A survey of Nonconformist activity made in 1669 reported him as preaching to a congregation of no less than eight hundred Presbyterians in Spitalfields, 'at a New House built for that purpose, with Pulpit & Seates'. In this meeting house, with its 'three good galleries', Dr Annesley was licensed as a Presbyterian 'teacher' in 1672, when the Declaration of Indulgence officially allowed Nonconformists to worship in public.[1] Here he ministered until his death in 1696, though his long and fruitful ministry was subject to periodic disturbances, both religious and secular. The first of these was a reminder that the tumultuous religious passions roused under the Commonwealth were by no means extinct in the 1670s. On October the twentieth 1678, the service at Dr Annesley's new meeting house was interrupted by a Quakeress named Elizabeth Bathurst, who under conviction of the Spirit's leading, proceeded to vent the wrath of the Lamb upon the astonished congregation.

Elizabeth Bathurst and her sister Anne had both belonged to Annesley's Presbyterian congregation before joining the Friends. When Elizabeth failed to gain a satisfactory hearing at the meeting house where she had once worshipped, she published *An Expostulatory Appeal to the Professors of Christianity, Joyned in Community with Samuel Ansley*.[2] In this pamphlet she described, more in sorrow than in anger, the rebuff she had met with at their hands. She tried to speak during the service, but was asked 'to be silent during Prayer time' and wait till the end of the service. She duly waited,

---

[1] A. Gordon, *Freedom after Ejection*, (1917), p. 201.
[2] No date; a copy is in the Library of the Friends' Historical Society.

but 'no sooner had I charged you with being out of the right way, but you made good that charge immediately, by shew-ing that persecuting Spirit, which infallibly marks out and deciphers the false Church'. In other words, they promptly showed her the door. She had approached Dr Annesley personally, 'to render the Reason of my turning from him', but received only 'a hasty Put-by from him'. No doubt he found it hard to deal with this sincere but volatile woman, who while professing 'a kind and friendly Respect' for him, denounces him and his flock as 'found in the Spirit of Antichrist'.[1]

On Saturday November the eighteenth 1682, Dr Annesley suffered a disturbance of a different kind when his house was raided and his goods seized to pay fines incurred by conduct-ing Nonconformist worship. The Declaration of Indulgence (1672) had been revoked the following year, and sporadic persecution of the Dissenters began again. A contemporary chronicle of events recorded laconically that, 'Dr Ansleys house was broke into by the Informers &c. on Saturday & his Goods distrained upon for severall latent Convictions.'[2] Such a raid was often a vicious affair, in which the constables, incited by the informers, ransacked a man's house and plundered his goods far beyond the limit of the legal fine. Not that the fines were negligible. One London minister in this very year was fined £840 for holding meetings, and even Dr Annesley's private means cannot have stood such losses for long.[3]

The period 1682-3, brought two further personal blows to Dr Annesley, through the actions of his daughters. One was married without his knowledge to the infamous Thomas Dangerfield, one of the informers involved in the Popish Plot. He was impartial in his malice, and would inform

---

[1] Elizabeth Bathurst, *An Expostulatory Appeal*, pp. 4–5.
[2] Dr. Williams' Library, Morrice MSS, Entering Book, Vol. 1, f. 345.
[3] For full details, see G. R. Cragg, *Puritanism in the period of the Great Persecution 1660–1688*, (1957), pp. 56ff.

against Presbyterians as well as Catholics, having drawn up in 1679, 'a paper concerning pretended clubs or meetings of the presbyterians, with full lists of the members of each'.[1] Under 7 April 1683, a contemporary record noted, 'Mr Dangerfield some time since married Dr Annesley's daughter without her father's knowledge, and about the beginning of last weeke claimed her and has her', adding, what we may well believe, 'it makes a great deale of discourse in town.'[2] Yet what was to the town a passing scandal, must have been to Dr Annesley an enduring shame and sorrow.

The second family upset at this period was the decision of his young daughter, Susanna, not yet thirteen, to return to the Church of England. We shall look more fully at this crucial turning point in her life, and suggest some possible reasons for it, in the next chapter. Here we need only say that Dr Annesley, whose feelings can be imagined, accepted Susanna's decision with a quite extraordinary charity and understanding.[3] This reaction is an index of the strength of Annesley's Christian character, a character which neither ecclesiastical reversals nor personal misfortune could sour. He remained active and hopeful to the end. His son-in-law, John Dunton, compared him to St Paul, and described how, 'He had the care of all the Churches upon his mind, and was the great support of Dissenting Ministers, and of the Morning Lecture.' He was also one of the Managers of the 'Common Fund' set up jointly in 1690 by Presbyterians and Congregationalists for the support of needy ministers and congregations. He made a personal contribution of a hundred pounds, and promised to continue it as an annual subscription.[4] In 1694 he took part in the first public ordination service for a Nonconformist minister to be held in London since 1662, at his own meeting-house. Yet

---

[1] See *D.N.B.*, s.v. Thomas Dangerfield.
[2] Dr Williams' Library, Morrice MSS, Entering Book, Vol. I, f. 363.
[3] See below, pp. 61f.
[4] A. Gordon, *Freedom after Ejection*, pp. 158ff.

neither his responsibilities nor his sorrows could overwhelm him, and John Dunton could write from personal knowledge, 'His Nonconformity created him many troubles; however, all the difficulties and disappointments he met with from an ungrateful world did never alter the goodness and the cheerfulness of his humour.'[1] In the last year of Dr Annesley's life, 1696, there was published the autobiography of his old friend, Richard Baxter. It contained, as part of a 'Description of the London Ministers', a characterization of Annesley: 'Dr Annesley is a most sincere, godly, humble Man, totally devoted to God, worthily to be joyned with his two great intimate Friends, Dr Drake, and Mr White, whose Preaching in those two greatest Auditories, Giles's Cripplegate, and Paul's Church, did very much good till he was silenced.'[2] Silenced he may have been in the pulpits of St Paul's and St Giles', but he continued to proclaim the Word committed to him at his ordination, in his family, in his meeting-house, and through his books.

In outlining the career of Dr Annesley, we have incidentally gone some way towards sketching his character also. He stands out as a man of principle and integrity, devoted to his calling, and unswervingly loyal to his conscience. To fill out the picture, we can draw on a variety of sources of information. The first group consists of personalia bearing the impress of his character: portraits, a copy of the sale catalogue of his library, and, most notably, his own writings. The second group comprises descriptions of his character published by his friends and contemporaries. Of these, the two fullest are the funeral sermon preached by his friend Dr Daniel Williams,[3] and a 'Character' of Annesley

---

[1] Dunton, *Life and Errors*, I, 165.

[2] Baxter, *Reliquiae Baxterianae*, ed. Matthew Sylvester (1696), Pt. III, 95. Baxter wrote this part of his life in 1670. For a letter from Baxter to 'my Reverend & worthy friend Dr Annesley', dated 13 January 1678–9, see Dr Williams' Library MSS, Baxter Letters, Vol. II, f. 51.

[3] Daniel Williams, *The Excellency of A Publick Spirit: Set forth in a Sermon preach'd . . . at the Funeral of that late Reverend Divine Dr Samuel Annesley*, (1697).

in the form of an elegy, from the pen of Daniel Defoe,[1] who had sat in his congregation and paints a lively picture of him as pastor and preacher.

There are three known portraits or engravings of Dr Annesley, all in Dr Williams' Library.[2] Two are rather nondescript, sparing in detail, and showing him with a round, full face. The third, a fine portrait in oils, is much more interesting and distinctive. It shows him dressed in a skull-cap, gown, and preaching bands, with a lean, strong face, framed in long, black, curling hair. It is a manly face, full of strength and determination, and serves to remind us that Annesley had seen action as a naval chaplain. It does not so readily suggest the face of a scholar, but the testimony of friends and the evidence of his library combine to show that he was in fact a close student and a well-read divine. His library was large and impressive in its breadth: the Fathers, Greek and Latin, together with Roman Catholic, Anglican, and Nonconformist divinity, filled his shelves. Edward Millington, who auctioned his books on Thursday, 18th March 1697, at Rolls' Auction House in Petty Canon Alley near St Paul's, urged upon readers of his catalogue of the Annesley Library the worth both of the Doctor and his books:

This Catalogue consists of the Library of the Reverend and Learned Dr Annesley, lately deceas'd, a Person so Eminent for his Piety and Usefulness, being generally known, and universally esteem'd in this City, that I forbear any farther Character. I presume I may without Offence say, That the Books are considerable, and well chosen, being the best that cou'd be bought,

---

[1] *The Character of the late Dr Samuel Annesley, By way of Elegy . . . Written by one of his Hearers.* The Preface is signed 'D.F.', and John Dunton (*Life and Errors,* I, 166) confirms that these are in fact the initials of Daniel (de) Foe: 'After his decease, Mr Williams preached his Funeral Sermon, and Mr De Foe drew his Character, which I published. . . .' On Defoe's personal piety, partly no doubt formed under Annesley's ministry, see G. H. Healey, *The Meditations of Daniel Defoe* (1946).

[2] The engravings are found in a folio volume of illustrations to W. Wilson's *History of the Dissenting Churches of London,* (4 vols., 1808).

and generally Valu'd in his time. The Fathers, the best Editions, both Greek and Latin, that are extant; Church-History and Councils, valuable; School-men and Casuists, not common; The Commentators and Practical Expositors, Authors of great Repute (if not of Prime Note) when he purchas'd them. Philology, Humanity in Greek and Latin, not many, but very scarce. The whole is Inviting to all Studious and Knowing Persons, and will appear so, in the Perusing of the Catalogue, as also upon the View of the Books Three Days before the Sale.[1]

To the critical professional eye of Millington, some of Dr Annesley's books no doubt seemed rather out of date. They were 'the best that cou'd be bought, and generally Valu'd in his time'. Books, and not least theological books, date quickly, and some of the tomes from Dr Annesley's library published in the early and mid-seventeenth century would assuredly not find a very ready sale in 1697. Yet discounting the economics of book-selling—something Millington could hardly afford to do—it is clear that Dr Annesley had amassed a fine collection of books during his ministry of more than half a century.

Nor were his books simply so much study furniture. He really read them, as his writings show. Here the works listed in Millington's sale catalogue appear again, thumbed and used, cited and criticized, as part of a minister's working library and not of a neatly classified inventory. Writing on 'What it is to love God with the whole heart', he refers, within a page or so, to the Fathers (Augustine, Gregory of Nyssa, and Origen), to Anselm the scholastic, to John Gerhard the Lutheran, and to Cajetan the Roman Catholic controversialist.[2] The copious marginal references in his books reveal the breadth of his learning, and yet it was learning put to extremely practical use. Most of his

---

[1] *Bibliotheca Annesliana : or a Catalogue of Choice Greek, Latin, and English Books, both Ancient and Modern . . . being the Library of the Reverend Samuel Annesley, L.L.D. And Minister of the Gospel Lately Deceas'd.* (S.C. 881 in the British Museum collection of Catalogues of British Book Sales.)

[2] *A Supplement to the Morning-Exercise at Cripplegate,* ed. Sam. Annesley, 2nd ed. (1676), pp. 4–5.

31

published work consists of sermons: the sermon before the
Commons, funeral sermons for his friends, sermons at the
Morning Exercises. Like his grandson, John Wesley, whom a
recent writer has described as 'the last of the Puri ı
divines',[1] Dr Annesley was 'a great preacher to the conscience'.[2] His normal preaching dealt with 'cases of conscience', or practical matters of Christian conduct and belief.
At the Morning Exercises he handled such questions as, 'How
may we be universally and exactly conscientious?', 'How
may we attain to love God?', and 'How may we give Christ
a satisfying account why we attend upon the ministry of the
Word?' In the words of his friend, Daniel Williams, 'By his
very often reading over the Scriptures from his Childhood, he
became a great Textuary; and by aptly produced Texts, he
oft surprised eminent Ministers; as his solution of Cases of
Conscience (which his Sermons much consisted of) did
instruct and satisfie them.'[3] Daniel Defoe concurs as to the
essential bent of his learning: 'Practical Divinity was his
Business, and Cases of Conscience his Study.'[4]

As a preacher, Annesley had the gift of presenting Christian
truth at once attractively and with a searching personal
application. Defoe shows him in action in the pulpit:

> The SACRED BOW he so Divinely drew,
> That every shot both hit and overthrew;
> His native Candor, and familiar Stile,
> Which did so oft his Hearers Hours beguile,
> Charm'd us with Godliness, and while he spake,
> We lov'd the Doctrine for the Teacher's sake.
> While he inform'd us what his Doctrines meant,
> By dint of Practice more than Argument,
> Strange were the Charms of his Sincerity,

[1] Horton Davies, *Worship and Theology in England from Watts and Wesley to
Maurice, 1690–1850*, (1961), p. 184.
[2] J. H. Rigg, *The Living Wesley*, pp. 128–9; quoted by Horton Davies,
op. cit., p. 156n.
[3] D. Williams, *The Excellency of a Publick Spirit*, p. 139.
[4] D.F., *The Character of the Late Dr Samuel Annesley*, Preface.

> Which made his Actions and his Words agree
> At such a constant and exact a rate,
> As made a Harmony we wondred at . . .[1]

Part of his attractiveness as a preacher no doubt sprang from his skilful use of the homely illustration. With a few deft strokes he could drive his point home sharply and memorably. Preaching on conscience, he argues that even 'practical Atheists', who reject God, 'yet cannot get rid of his Deputy, their Conscience', and adds, 'Those that are without or Reject the Sunshine of Scripture, yet they cannot blow out Gods Candle of Conscience'.[2] In the same sermon he likens conscience to a sleepy, fretful child: 'O how often hath thy Conscience whimper'd, and thou hast husht it to sleep again! What doth thy sleepy Conscience most dread? an awakening Ministry? So far cross thy Conscience as to attend no other: Instead of lullaby notions, improve cutting convictions.' In his treatment of 'A scrupulous Conscience', he has another neat simile: 'A scruple in the minde is as gravell in the shooe, it vexeth the Conscience as that hurts the foot.'[3]

Together with Dr Annesley's popular preaching style, there went an intense pastoral concern and zeal for souls. It was these very qualities that led many Nonconformists to supply the places of parish clergy who fled from London when the horror of the Great Plague struck the city in 1665. Puritans then mounted the steps of pulpits left empty by their incumbents, and ministered to the sick and dying in the stricken city.[4] Of Samuel Annesley's activities during the Plague Year, we have no direct knowledge; but of his pastoral concern and devotion, there is evidence from more than one source. We see it in the pastoral letter with which

[1] Ibid., pp. 6–7.
[2] *The Morning-Exercise at Cripplegate*, ed. Annesley (1661), p. 5.
[3] Ibid., pp. 10, 17 (2).
[4] For contemporary references, see Cragg, *Puritanism in the Period of the Great Persecution, 1660–1688*, p. 13, and Defoe, *A Journal of the Plague Year* (1927 ed.), p. 32.

B

he prefaced the first volume of sermons preached at the Morning Exercise:

To my most unfeignedly Beloved Parishioners of Saint GILES Cripplegate.
My Dear Friends,
These Sermons, both preach'd and printed are the meer product of love to your Souls. I never yet (that I remember) went thorow the Parish without some (though not sutably compassionate) heart-akeing yearnings towards my charge. to think (and oh that I could think of it according to the worth of Souls) how many thousands here are posting to Eternity, that within a few years will be in Heaven or Hell, and I know not how, so much as to ask them whither they are going . . .[1]

We see the high conception of the ministerial office, a sure token of the true Puritan, which lay behind this pastoral concern, in his funeral sermon for the Reverend William Whitaker, preached in 1673. Whitaker, says Annesley, embodied the truth that, 'A Minister's whole being should be in his Ministry; his soul, his body, his time, all his graces, all his learning, all his studies, all his interests, all laid out in the work of THE Ministry.' He goes on to stir up his fellow-ministers to emulate Whitaker in the exercise of their ministry: 'Lets make it our business to be as much Ministers out of the Pulpit, as in it. The well discharge of the Ministry is an intolerable drudgery to a carnal heart: to have not our Sermons, but our occasional discourses; to have not only our words, but our silence speak us Ministers of Christ; to be always upon our watch (if I may so speak) sleeping and waking, that is, to sleep no more than is necessary to our watchfulness; who that is not gracious (I had almost said) eminently gracious, can endure it?'[2]

Annesley's own words are endorsed by the testimony of those who knew him well. Timothy Rogers, preaching at the funeral of Annesley's daughter Elizabeth, who did not long

[1] *The Morning-Exercise at Cripplegate*, ed. Annesley (1661), Preface.
[2] Annesley, *A Sermon Preached at the Funeral of Reverend Mr Will. Whitaker* (1673), pp. 24ff.

survive her father, calls to mind his having 'so flaming and so hearty a Love to the Salvation of Men'. As the funeral was being held in Annesley's meeting-house, Rogers could confidently assert, 'I know there are among you several that bless God for him, and who love everything that's any way related to so tender and so good a Man. This Pulpit, and these Seats, and all you have been Witnesses of his Fervour: he never spared his Body, nor his Pains to do you good; many an hour in secret did he pray for you, as well as many an hour he spent in very diligent and severe Studies, to do you good.'[1] John Dunton, the eccentric printer and bookseller who married Elizabeth Annesley, paid a similar tribute to his father-in-law: 'Among my Dissenting Authors, I shall begin with Dr Annesley, a man of wonderful Piety and Humility. I have heard him say, that "He never knew the time he was not converted". The great business and the pleasure of his life was, "to persuade sinners back to God from the general apostacy"; and in the faithful discharge of his Ministry he spent fifty-five years.'[2] While on a business trip to America in 1686, Dunton received striking confirmation of Dr Annesley's evangelical zeal. He was visiting places of interest in New England, and having seen Harvard College, of which Annesley's friend Richard Baxter was a benefactor, he records:

My next ramble was to Roxbury, in order to visit the Rev. Mr Elliot, the great Apostle of the Indians. He was pleased to receive me with abundance of respect; and inquired very kindly after Dr Annesley, my Father-in-law, and then broke out with a world of seeming satisfaction, 'Is my brother Annesley yet alive? Is he yet converting souls to God? Blessed be God for this information before I die.' He presented me with twelve Indian Bibles, and desired me to bring one of them over to Dr Annesley; as also with twelve 'Speeches of converted Indians', which himself had published.[3]

[1] Timothy Rogers, *The Character of a Good Woman* (1697), pp. 122ff.
[2] Dunton, *Life and Errors*, I, 165.
[3] Dunton, op. cit., I, 115.

The saintly Puritan John Eliot (1604–1690) was nearing the end of a noble life and ministry when Dunton met him in 1686. His gifts and graces were in many ways similar to those of Dr Annesley himself, and his sterling character gives his words of commendation real weight. Richard Baxter said of Eliot, 'There was no man on earth whom I honour'd above him,' while a modern biographical sketch suggests a singularly impressive and attractive character:

He was the first to carry the gospel to the red man, and perhaps the earliest who championed the negro. Strangers with whom he came in contact spoke of the peculiar charm of his manners. He united fervent piety and love of learning to burning enthusiasm for evangelisation, these qualities being tempered with worldly wisdom and shrewd common sense . . . No name in the early history of New England is more revered than his. Eliot was truly of a saintly type, without fanaticism, spiritual pride, or ambition.[1]

A final tribute to Dr Annesley's capacity as pastor and evangelist, comes from Edmund Calamy, who is defending him against an opponent who alleged that Annesley was unlearned and quite undeserving of his doctorate. Calamy rejoined, 'Whatever he was for a Civilian (i.e. a Civil Lawyer) his Works will witness for him that he was a Good Divine, and a considerable Casuist. And if Solomon's Maxim that he that winneth Souls is wise, may be allow'd to stand good, Dr Annesley must be own'd to have been one of more than common Wisdom.'[2]

With this intense pastoral concern, Dr Annesley united acute spiritual insight in the cure of souls. Puritanism at its best excelled in this insight, which received classic expression in Baxter's *Autobiography*.[3] We find the same quality in a sermon of Annesley's on conscience, where he gives detailed

[1] *D.N.B.*, s.v. John Eliot.

[2] Calamy, *Continuation*, I, 72. For the quite unsubstantiated charge of 'Egregious Stupidity', made against Annesley by John Walker, to whom Calamy is replying, see Walker, *Sufferings of the Clergy*, (1714), Pt. II, 39.

[3] Compare especially, Baxter, *Autobiography*, ed. Lloyd Thomas, pp. 103–132 (Baxter's 'Self-analysis and Life-review').

and pertinent advice to the man with a 'trembling conscience', who has fears for his soul's state. First, says Annesley, 'Bless God for an awakened conscience.' Then, 'Observe 'tis Gods usuall method to bring the soul through these perplexities to the most solid spirituall peace.' Finally, in the sphere of action, he counsels, 'Do but hold on in the vigorous use of all means of Grace, and reckon Gods keeping thee from turning thy back on his ways, when thou hast no comfort in them, the secret supports he gives, which thou tak'st no notice of.'[1]

All his pastoral zeal and spiritual insight, however, were tempered by a humble modesty. In both theology and churchmanship he seems to have been, like his friend Richard Baxter, of a notably moderate and irenical spirit. It is surely significant that such a leading divine as Dr Annesley should have left behind him no contributions to the fierce theological warfare of his day, no controversial tracts and pamphlets instinct with the *odium theologicum*. He was content to be preacher, pastor, casuist; controversy he left to others. Not that he lacked openings, if he had been looking for personal matters of dispute, for his doctorate, his relationship to the Earl of Anglesey, his sermon before the Commons, and his dealings with the Quakers, all made him the subject of attack, sometimes in print. Yet he never replied in kind,—almost as though he were too preoccupied with his ministry to spend time wiping off the personal slurs which were cast upon him. It was not merely lack of time, however. He positively eschewed controversy. In a preface he contributed to Richard Allein's *Instruction about Heart-Work* (1684), he expressed a fervent wish that the only contention among Christians might be over who could do most to promote personal religion: 'Were all our swords of contention beaten into plough-shares and pruning-hooks, for ploughing up the fallow ground of the heart, for pulling up the weeds, and

[1] *The Morning-Exercise at Cripplegate*, ed. Annesley, p. 18 (2).

cutting off the luxuriances of the heart; were it the only contention, who should most promote gracious heart-work in themselves and others; it would afford comfort both living and dying.'

We may gauge Annesley's own disposition even more clearly from the tributes included in the funeral sermon he preached for his friend and convert, Thomas Brand. He extolled Brand as a minister whose 'chief Zeal was neither for, nor against any Party whatsoever, but for the vigorous Promoting of the sound Knowledge of those Doctrines wherein we are all agreed, and of that Holiness which we all commend, tho' too few practice: And this right Christian Temper he exercised towards the Conforming Clergy. He spake honourably of the Piety and Learning of some, and never let fly indecent Reflections, or bitter Invectives against any, but maintained and encreased this Commendable Moderation all his Life'.[1] And so, we may be reasonably certain, did Dr Annesley. Defoe referred to him as, 'Dr ANNESLEY, whose generous Soul had nothing in him that was little or mean,' and grew warm in praise of, 'the Zeal, the Candor, the Sincerity of his Mind; the Largeness of his Charity, the Greatness of his Soul, the Sweetness of his Temper, and the Vastness of his Designs to propagate the Kingdom and Interest of his Master.'[2] In the same vein, Daniel Williams was moved by the life of Annesley to urge those who attended his funeral to 'an intentness to promote mere Christianity, and unaffected Godliness, which reforms the world, edifies the Church, and saves the Souls of Sinners in proportion to its success.' Annesley's whole life was a rebuke to 'a narrow Sectarian Spirit', by which, said Williams, 'I mean a Spirit that confineth Charity to a Sect distinguished from other Christians, by Customs or Opinions

[1] Annesley, *The Life and Funeral Sermon of the Reverend Mr Thomas Brand*, (1692), p. 3.
[2] D. F., *The Character of the late Dr Samuel Annesley*, Preface.

that are not essential to true Godliness, and is embittered and enraged against all who differ from such Usages and Opinions. This is the Spirit of Popery; (which is a Sect, tho' a great one). . . .'[1]

Here we breathe the same atmosphere as in the writings of Richard Baxter, who in ecclesiastical controversy was a consistent champion of the Augustinian formula for peace, 'Unity in things necessary and liberty in things unnecessary, and charity in all,' and who confessed, 'I am much more sensible than ever of the necessity of living upon the principles of religion which we are all agreed in, and uniting these; and how much mischief men that overvalue their own opinions have done by their controversies in the Church; how some have destroyed charity, and some caused schisms by them, and most have hindered godliness in themselves and others, and used them to divert men from the serious prosecuting of a holy life.'[2]

To charity and tolerance, Dr Annesley added humility and modesty. His humility was indeed one of the qualities which most impressed those who knew him intimately. Baxter's description of Annesley as 'a most sincere, godly, humble man', was echoed by Defoe, who called him, 'A Moses for Humility and Zeal', and averred:

> Humility was his dear and darling Grace,
> And Honesty sate Regent in his Face;
> Meekness of Soul did in his Aspect shine,
> But in the truth, resolv'd and masculine.[3]

John Dunton similarly testified that he was 'a man of wonderful Piety and Humility',[4] and Daniel Williams

---

[1] Williams, *The Excellency of A Publick Spirit*, p. 64.

[2] Baxter, *Autobiography*, ed. Lloyd Thomas, pp. 91, 106. For other examples of this irenical and ecumenical spirit in Nonconformity, see William Bates, *A Funeral Sermon . . . upon . . . Dr Thomas Manton* (1678), pp. 55f; Isaac Watts's Preface to John Reynolds, *A Practical Discourse of Reconciliation* (1729), p. viii; and Isaac Watts, *Orthodoxy and Charity United* (1745), pp. 94, 266, 281f.

[3] D.F., *The Character of the late Dr Samuel Annesley*, p. 9.

[4] Dunton, *Life and Errors*, I, 165.

concurred: 'His humility was signal. He seemed to have the meanest Opinion of his own Gifts and Labours.'[1]

Enough has been said to show that there was more than a touch of the 'catholic spirit' of John Wesley in his grandfather's life and character. Nor does the resemblance end there. We may be sure that Annesley's grandson would have kindled to the old Puritan's pursuit of 'downright godliness'. When we hear Annesley pleading for, 'an humble, serious, constant course of godliness,'[2] we are reminded of Wesley's persistent quest for holiness of heart and life, and of his passion for Christianity in earnest. This likeness is most strikingly seen in a remarkable passage from one of Dr Annesley's sermons, which might well have been written by John Wesley, who did in fact reprint it in his *Christian Library*. As we hear Annesley's words, it might almost be Wesley expounding that master text which for him embraced the whole dimension of Christian living, 'Faith working by love'. The passage runs:

Remember these two words, though you forget all the rest of the Sermon, *viz.*, 'CHRIST and Holiness, Holiness and CHRIST': interweave these all manner of ways, in your whole conversation. . . .

It is serious Christianity that I press, as the only way to better every condition: it is Christianity, downright Christianity, that alone can do it: it is not morality without faith; that is but refined Heathenism: it is not faith without morality: that is but downright hypocrisy: it must be a divine faith, wrought by the HOLY GHOST, where GOD and man concur in the operation; such a faith as works by love, both to GOD and man; a holy faith, full of good works.[3]

In Annesley, as in Wesley, we find the same stress on love of God as the supreme motive force of Christian living;[4] the same emphasis upon duty—Annesley's first prescription for

[1] Williams, *The Excellency of a Publick Spirit*, p. 142.
[2] *A Supplement to the Morning-Exercise at Cripplegate*, ed. Annesley (1674), Preface to the Reader.
[3] *A Christian Library*, ed. John Wesley, (30 vols., 1819–27), XXIV, 453f.
[4] See below, p. 134.

a good conscience is, 'Consult duty not events. There's nothing in the world for us to do, but to mind our duty,'[1]— and upon method; the same concern for Christian perfection; the same insistence upon the means of grace. In temperament too, in their common charm of manner, their generous temper and irenical spirit, it would appear to be a case of like grandfather, like grandson. This hereditary influence and family likeness was transmitted to Wesley through his mother, who was the child of a Puritan home. Having looked at her father's life and personality, we must now try to understand in greater detail exactly what was involved in the Puritan upbringing which helped to shape his daughter so decisively.

[1] *The Morning-Exercise at Cripplegate*, ed. Annesley, p. 23 (2).

CHAPTER TWO

The Puritan Maid

There's no Time for preparing for Heaven like the
Time of Youth. Tho Death were never so near, I can
look back with Joy on some of the early years that I
sweetly spent in my Father's House, and how I comfortably lived there. O what a Mercy it is to be
Dedicated to God betimes! *Elizabeth Annesley*

THESE words of her sister Elizabeth,[1] spoken on
her death-bed, were echoed by Susanna, as she too in her
turn looked back to the early years which she had sweetly
spent in her father's house. Her Puritan home and upbringing set a stamp upon her which she never lost, exercised a
formative influence on her piety and devotion, and are vital
for any true understanding of the way in which she later
managed her own household at Epworth.

Her father had a large brood of children, having, in the
pious metaphor of John Dunton, 'produced much fruit for
Heaven!' Dunton continued his reminiscence of his father-
in-law, 'I heard him say, "he has had twenty-five children".

[1] Rogers, *Character of a Good Woman*, p. 158.

43

Dr Manton baptizing one of them, and being asked how many Children the Doctor had, he returned this answer: "that he believed it was two dozen, or a quarter of a hundred;" which reckoning of children by dozens was a thing so very uncommon, that I have heard Dr Annesley mention it with a special remark.'[1]

Susanna was the youngest child, and far more is known of her than of any of her numerous brothers and sisters. For the most part even their names have perished, but the scattered references to the Annesley children which have come down to us suggest a spirited and lively family. Samuel Annesley junior grew rich in the service of the East India Company, and in 1724 had planned to sail for England and bring home his wealth. Susanna left her family at Epworth, and made the long journey to London to meet his ship, only to find no sign of him on board. She returned home, presuming him dead, in circumstances which gave strong suggestion of foul play.[2] Benjamin, the only other brother whose name is known, was intending, at the time of his father's death, to follow him into the ministry. This knowledge proved a great comfort to his devout sister Elizabeth in her last illness: 'It was a great Support to her to think that her Brother Benjamin was design'd for a Minister, and she hoped that God would (as her Father was confident he would) use him as an Instrument to promote his Glory, and the Good of Souls.'[3]

Elizabeth Annesley was the sister whom Susanna most closely resembled, both in person and character, so that, as Eliza Clarke infers, 'anything recorded of Mrs Dunton (i.e. Elizabeth) throws a side light on Mrs Wesley's character.'[4] Elizabeth early showed the temper of piety and

---

[1] Dunton, *Life and Errors*, I, 166. For Dr Thomas Manton, (1620–77), a Presbyterian colleague of Dr Annesley, see *D.N.B.* s.v. Manton. Annesley had two wives, but the second bore twenty-four of his children, including Susanna.

[2] For a full account, see Clarke, *Wesley Family*, I, 381f.

[3] Rogers, *Character of a Good Woman*, p. 149.

[4] Eliza Clarke, *Susanna Wesley*, p. 24f.

goodness which was to be hers until the day she died. According to Timothy Rogers, her father used to say that she 'never displeased him in all his life'. For her part, Elizabeth acknowledged 'the good Providence of God, in giving her Religious Parents, that with United Endeavours, took a mighty Care of her Education; and she was good when she was very Young. She found her heart changed to the Love of the Best Things, but when she did not particularly know; as is the Case of many Children of Good People, into whom Goodness is instilled by Degrees, and who find themselves alive, though they do not know the first moment, when they began to live. She received with her Father the Holy Sacrament of the Lord's Supper, between Fifteen and Sixteen; betimes it seems had she fortified her self against the Pomps and Vanities of the World by the Sight of a Crucified Jesus.'[1] As a result of this careful religious training, she grew up, like Susanna herself, an informed and balanced Christian, devoted to prayer and meditation, sermon and sacrament. She married in 1682 a young London printer and bookseller named John Dunton. Dunton was undoubtedly something of a fool, but an amiable one. There was a Boswellian streak of vanity and ostentation in him, and large sections of his rambling autobiography consist of lists of well-known people —divines, politicians, and booksellers—whom he boasted of numbering among his friends. He was unbelievably indiscreet, and frequently printed private and personal correspondence to fill out his story, so that one exasperated acquaintance wrote him an acid note in 1718, informing him, 'You will hear no more from me, and I desire you would write no more to me without I give you new directions. There is no writing to a man that prints everything.'[2] Yet odd and unpredictable as he was, Dunton remains an attractive character. He had a genuine feeling for religion, and his

[1] Rogers, *Character of a Good Woman*, p. 126f.
[2] Dunton, *Life and Errors*, I, xxx.

Life and Errors is suffused by his own peculiar brand of Puritan piety. His bookselling flourished, despite his misadventures, and he and Elizabeth were to live happily together.

Dunton first met his future wife, when as a young apprentice he slipped one Sunday into Dr Annesley's meeting-house, and, thanks to a sight of one of the Annesley girls, had the utmost difficulty in concentrating on the sermon. 'One Lord's-day (and I am very sensible of the sin) I was strolling about just as my fancy led me; and stepping into Dr Annesley's Meeting-place, where, instead of engaging my attention to what the Doctor said, I suffered both my mind and my eyes to run at random . . . I soon singled out a young lady that almost charmed me dead; but, having made my inquiries, I found to my sorrow she was pre-engaged. However, my Friends, to keep up the humour I was in, advised me to make an experiment upon her elder Sister (they both being the Daughters of the Reverend Dr Annesley); and the hint they gave me, as Providence would have it, made a deeper impression upon me than all the recommendations they had given me before . . .' He went ahead and secured Dr Annesley's permission—after his master, Mr Parkhurst, had vouched for his character—to sue for the hand of his daughter: 'The Doctor told me, I had his free consent, if I could prevail upon his Daughter for hers; which was more than Mr Cockeril (deceased) could ever obtain, after a long courtship.' Dunton fared better than the late Mr Cockeril, won Elizabeth's consent, and so embarked on, 'the greatest happiness I have as yet met with in this life.'[1]

In the summer of 1682, Elizabeth had to accompany her father to Tunbridge Wells, apparently so that Dr Annesley might take the waters for his health. On July 6th, an impatient Dunton wrote to her from London a gallant love-letter, using the romantic pseudonymns Iris and Philaret,

[1] Dunton, *Life and Errors*, I, 64–5.

46

and begging, 'Why will not you write a long Letter? Nay, lovely Iris, let me have one from you as large as a Folio; nothing can drop from your pen, but will give poor languishing Philaret all the transports that a Lover can imagine.' In her reply 'Iris' brings him down to earth and reveals the fruit of her Puritan training, in deprecating his extravagant expressions:

Tunbridge, July 9, 1682

Dear Sir,

I have received your Letters; but, being obliged to take a small journey from Tunbridge with my Father, I had no opportunity to make you any answer. You seem impatient at my silence, but it is only a matter of course; though were your impatience represented with less of fancy, I should be disposed to believe you sooner. But all Courtships must, at one time or other, have a little Knight-errantry in them, otherwise, the Lover is reckoned to be something dull; however, you have said enough that way to secure you from any such imputation, and I would have you express yourself in no warmer terms than a primitive simplicity may admit of. One that loves till he loses his reason, will make but an odd figure for a husband. You will say, perhaps, I am preaching up passive obedience; but we shall agree upon that point afterwards. At present please to deny yourself a little luxuriance in your Letters, lest my Father should find them, and be offended with them.[1]

Poor Dunton can hardly have been gratified at having his ardours quenched in this matter-of-fact way, and yet, temperamentally inclined to hyperbole as he was, he probably needed this mild reproof. What is more interesting in Elizabeth's letter is her attachment to her father, and the thorough way in which she had learned the lesson of 'primitive simplicity', which her Puritan home had taught her. Her objection to Dunton's flowery epistles was no mere petty scrupulosity. It sprang basically from a strict Puritan regard for truth, and Puritan love of the simple, plain, decent, comely, in speech as in all else.

Lest it be thought that the home in which the Annesley

[1] Dunton, op. cit., I, 67–8.

girls grew up was rather severe, and somewhat lacking in human warmth and feeling, we may look at the sermon which Dr Annesley preached on the occasion of Elizabeth's marriage to John Dunton, at Allhallows the Wall, on August 3rd 1682.[1] We hear Dr Annesley expatiating upon the joys of married love, with real tenderness and understanding. Preaching from Ephesians 5: 32 ('This is a great mystery . . .'), he stressed that, 'The Duties of the Married State must be performed, if the Comforts of it be expected,' and then continued, according to Dunton's summary, in the following way:

Under this head the several duties were insisted upon at large; but the necessity of Love, as the fundamental article, was clearly argued, from which all the other duties would follow, out of inclination and choice. The motive to it was the innocence of pleasure. Prov. v. 19. 'Be thou always ravished with her Love.' The place would answer the original much better, were it read, 'Err thou always in her Love;' as if it were said, this degree of love would be an Error in any other case, but here thou mayest err, and yet be innocent; here thou mayest roam, and wander, and lose thyself, and yet not sin; it must be a nonsuch-love.[2]

Besides Elizabeth, three more of Susanna's sisters are known to us by name, Sarah, Judith, and Anne. Sarah is little more than a name, unfortunately. Judith, like Susanna, combined good looks with a pious disposition. She never married, though not because she lacked a suitor. She refused the man who wanted to marry her, on the ground that he was 'addicted to much wine'.[3] This fact alone might warrant the inference that Judith Annesley also had responded positively to her Puritan upbringing; but John Dunton fills in the picture so as to make the point quite clear: 'She is a Virgin of eminent piety. Good Books (and, above all, the Book of Books) are her sweetest entertainment; and she finds

---

[1] Dunton, *Life and Errors*, I, 69, says the sermon was preached, (presumably at Dr Annesley's meeting-house), 'preparatory to the Marriage' at Allhallows.

[2] Ibid., I, 70.

[3] Clarke, *Wesley Family*, I, 395.

more comfort there than others do in their Dressing-room, or Wardrobe. In a word, she keeps a constant watch over the frame of her soul, and the course of her actions, by daily and strict examination of both.'[1] This last lesson of daily self-examination was one which Susanna also learned well, and practised to the end of her life. The two girls were good-looking as well as good, and Judith's beauty was set down on canvas by the hand of Sir Peter Lely. Yet a friend who knew them both commented that, 'beautiful as Miss Annesley appears, she was far from being as beautiful as Mrs Wesley.'[2] Finally, there was Anne Annesley, who is also favoured by a vignette from Dunton: 'She was the first (and happy) occasion of my being acquainted with dear Iris; and therefore to drop her pious Character would be ungrateful. She is a Wit for certain; and, however Time may have dealt by her, when I first beheld her, I thought Art never feigned, nor Nature formed, a finer Woman.'[3] The story that Anne married Daniel Defoe is now disproved,[4] or Dr Annesley would have been able to add yet another flamboyant son-in-law to the three his daughters brought him,—John Dunton, Thomas Dangerfield, and Samuel Wesley!

We might well infer, both from the descriptions of Dr Annesley's cheerful good nature, and from his children's happy reminiscences of their home, that the early years of Susanna and her brothers and sisters were filled with quiet joys and pleasure. At this point it will probably be objected that a puritanical home life is hardly consistent with a happy childhood. If Puritan homelife was uniformly marked by unsmiling austerity, the objection may be sustained; but was it? It is here that we must beware of the caricature of Puritanism fostered by scholars like Macaulay and Gardiner, and try to see Puritanism dispassionately as it was; for, as

[1] Dunton, *Life and Errors*, I, 355–6.
[2] Quoted by Stevenson, *Memorials of the Wesley Family*, p. 161.
[3] Dunton, *Life and Errors*, I, 354–5.
[4] See *Proceedings of the Wesley Historical Society*, XXIII, 23.

M. Henri Talon so pertinently reminds us, 'We must see the Puritan in his home if we really want to understand him: only then a whole legend collapses!'[1] M. Talon's sensitive and perceptive study of Bunyan has a far wider reference than the title suggests, and sheds a great deal of light on the inner meaning of Puritanism. Earlier in his book he shows the importance of Bunyan's understanding of the Church in terms of the home and family: 'The Palace Beautiful is the Church as Bunyan conceives it: a sort of *home* where one draws refreshment in communion with God and brotherly fellowship. His Church is social, if one can accept this use of the word.'[2]

If the Church was seen in terms of a home or family, as the household of faith, then the converse was also true, and for the Puritan the family was a microcosm of the Church. Home religion was quite central to Puritan piety, which was by no means focused solely upon the pulpit. John Geree, writing in 1646, and describing the character of an 'old English Puritan', said of him: 'His family he endeavoured to make a Church, both in regard of persons and exercises, admitting none into it but such as feared God; and labouring that those that were born in it, might be born again to God.'[3] That this Puritan emphasis had not become old-fashioned in the later seventeenth century, can be seen from the writings of Dr Annesley's friends and contemporaries. Geree's sentiments are echoed by Joseph Allein, who counsels, 'Let every family with you be a christian church, every house a house of prayer.'[4] Family religion is specifically dealt with in a number of the books of Annesley's friend Richard Baxter. In

---

[1] H. Talon, *John Bunyan, the man and his works* (E.T. 1951), p. 191. Talon's whole paragraph merits careful attention.

[2] Talon, op. cit., p. 149.

[3] John Geree, *The Character of an old English Puritane or Non-Conformist* (1646), p. 5. For further references to Puritan home life, see H. S. Porter, *Reformation and Reaction in Tudor Cambridge*, (1958), pp. 221ff.

[4] Joseph Allein, *A Counsel for Personal and Family Godliness*, as reprinted by John Wesley in his *Christian Library*, XIV, 174f.

The Reformed Pastor, he is quite adamant that ministers must pay special attention to catechizing families in their homes, and to 'instruction from house to house'. He is sure that religion will never be securely based until it is built into the very structure of family life: 'The life of religion, and the welfare and glory of church and state dependeth much on Family-government and duty . . . What are we like to do ourselves to the reforming of a congregation, if all the work be cast on us alone, and masters of families will let fall that necessary duty of their own, by which they are bound to help us!' He concludes: 'You are likely to see no general reformation till you procure family-reformation. Some little obscure religion there may be in here and there one; but while it sticks in single persons, and is not promoted by these societies, it doth not prosper, nor promise much for future increase.'[1]

If we may anticipate, Baxter's word here about 'general reformation' in the Church waiting upon 'family reformation', is strangely suggestive of the relation which Susanna's work at Epworth rectory was to bear to the Methodist Revival; and it is interesting that Baxter uses for the family the very term, 'society', which was later to denote the gatherings of the People called Methodists. Certainly John Wesley agreed with Baxter on the primary importance of family religion, which he called 'the grand desideratum among the Methodists'.[2] In his sermon *On Family Religion*, he argues that only if religion can be rooted in family life, will the Revival prove to be more than a passing phase: What will the consequence be . . . if family religion be neglected?—if care be not taken of the rising generation? Will not the present revival of religion in a short time die away?'[3]

[1] *The Practical Works of the Rev. Richard Baxter*, ed. W. Orme (23 vols., 1830), XIV, 97, 99.
[2] *The Journal of the Rev. John Wesley, A.M.*, ed. N. Curnock (8 vols., n.d., Preface 1909), V. 193 (entry for 16 Nov. 1767). Hereafter cited as *Journal*.
[3] Wesley, *Works*, ed. Thomas Jackson (14 vols., 1831), VII. 77.

Baxter returns to the same theme in a section of his great *Christian Directory* which he calls 'Christian Oeconomicks: or, The Family Directory'. He prefaces it with a note to 'all that fear God' in Kidderminster, where he had ministered for so long, and rejoices:

that once more before I dye, I have opportunity to speak to you at this distance, and to perswade you to, and Direct you in, that Family Holiness and Righteousness, which hath been so much of your Comfort and Honour, and will be so while you faithfully continue in it: O how happy a state is it, to have God dwell in your Families by his Love and Blessing, and rule them by his Word and Spirit, and Protect them by his Power, and delight in them and they in Him, as his Churches preparing for the Coelestial Delights! O how much of the Interest of true Religion must be kept up in the world, by the Holiness and Diligence of Christian Families![1]

We can be reasonably certain that Dr Annesley, who had Baxter's *Reformed Pastor*, *Christian Directory*, and *Poor Man's Family Book* (1674), on his shelves,[2] shared to the full his friend's concern for family religion. Besides Baxter's works, he kept within his study other works in the same field,—a *Parents Primmer*, Stockton's *Family Instruction*, Williams' *Vanity of Childhood*, and Lamb's *Religious Family*.[3] His concern for family religion shows in his sermon before the House of Commons in 1648, when one of the peremptory questions he rapped out at the members was, 'What are you in your Families? Are they well-ordered (little) Common-wealths, well disciplined Churches?'[4] That Dr Annesley tried to make his own family a well disciplined Church, we may gather from the tributes he paid to two of his ministerial friends. In a funeral sermon for William Whitaker, Dr Annesley commended him warmly for his 'relative piety', that is, his

---

[1] Baxter, *A Christian Directory* (1673), p. 473f.

[2] *Bibliotheca Annesleiana*, pp. 10, 13.

[3] Ibid., pp. 13ff.

[4] Annesley, *A Sermon preached to the Honourable House of Commons, July 26, 1648*, p. 23.

fostering of religion among his near relations. 'For his relative Piety, besides the family-duties that are common to all serious Christians, he kept a set-time of praying with his wife every day. And for his way of instructing, reproving, convincing, and counselling every person of his family, severally and privately in his Study as occasion required, praying with them ere he dismist them, that his words might abide; I never heard the like of any other.'[1] At another friend's funeral, Annesley quoted approvingly some words spoken on his death-bed: '. . . speaking to one about Family Prayer, he said, a Camel may as well go through the Eye of a Needle as a Man that prays not in his Family go to Heaven.'[2]

Susanna's father, then, fully shared the Puritan ideal of the family as a little gathered Church, where prayer, Bible-reading, catechizing, and detailed personal instruction in the Christian faith, provided a framework for the whole shared life of the home. How did Susanna react to such training? Her devotional writings and her letters provide part of the answer. Once, she confessed in her spiritual journal, she had been, 'discouraged by the experience of daily renewed failings,' and was tempted by doubt and fear to think that God might have cast her off. The grounds of her reassurance are significant. 'If he had been willing you should perish,' she told herself firmly, 'he might have let you have perished without the expense of so many miracles to save you. Why did he give you birth in a Christian Country, of Religious Parents, by whom you were early instructed in the principles of Religion? Why hath he waited so long to be gracious? Why hath his providence so often prevented you?'[3] Again, in a letter to her son John, dated 31 January 1727, having commended him for his thrift, she urged, 'Believe me, dear

[1] Annesley, *A Sermon Preached at the Funeral of Reverend Mr Will. Whitaker,* (1673), Preface to the Reader.
[2] Annesley, *The Life and Funeral Sermon of the Reverend Mr Thomas Brand,* (1692), p. 75.
[3] Headingley MSS, A.f.52.

son, old age is the worst time we can choose to mend either our lives or our fortunes. If the foundations of solid piety are not laid betimes in sound principles and virtuous dispositions; and if we neglect, while strength and vigour lasts, to lay up something ere the infirmities of age overtake us, it is a hundred to one odds that we shall die both poor and wicked.'[1] We may be confident that 'the foundations of solid piety' had been well and truly laid for Susanna in her earliest years; and the success of her father's training is most clearly seen in the thorough grounding in the Faith which she gave to her own children at Epworth.

The training continued for the boys even after they had left Epworth to go away to school. Susanna still guided and advised them by her letters, in which she gives revealing glimpses of her own childhood, as she addresses herself to the problems of theirs. Samuel, then a seventeen-year-old student at Westminster School, asked of his mother, 'some directions how to resist temptations', though without specifying the particular ways in which he was troubled. Susanna points out that this omission makes it difficult to give really detailed or helpful spiritual direction: 'You never informed me of any particular temptation to which you are exposed, and it is impossible from dark hints and general expressions to collect the true state of your case. Therefore I can but offer at general things; and if I happen to omit anything that I should chiefly insist on, I cannot help it.'[2] Nevertheless, she manages to give a good deal of shrewd advice about such typical temptations of a teenage boy as impure thoughts, neglect of prayer, over-eating or drinking, and finally over-indulgence in pleasure or recreation. It is under this last head that Susanna divulges to her son the way in which she had dealt with the claims of recreation in her girlhood:

[1] Clarke, *Wesley Family*, II, 23.
[2] Letter of 27 November 1707, printed in G. J. Stevenson, *Memorials of the Wesley Family*, p. 188.

The last instance of temperance in recreation I shall say little to. I do not know what time is assigned to you for it, and I think your health and studies require that you should use a pretty deal of exercise. You know whether your heart be too much set upon it. If it be, I will tell you what rule I observed in the same case when I was young and too much addicted to childish diversions, which was this: never to spend more time in any matter of mere recreation in one day than I spent in private religious duties. I leave it to your consideration whether this is practicable by you or not. I think it is.[1]

This passage is striking for the light it sheds, not only on her childhood, but on her method of spiritual direction. She does not dictate the moral decision to be made. She advises, she suggests a norm she had herself found helpful, but she leaves Samuel the moral and psychological space in which to make up his own mind.

Two years later, in the general context of the importance of redeeming the time—a typically Puritan emphasis—she repeated the same advice to 'Sammy':

First I would advise you, as much as is possible in your present circumstances, to throw all your business into a certain method, by which means you'll learn to improve every precious moment, and find an unspeakable facility in the performance of your respective duties. Begin and end the day with him who is the Alpha and Omega; and though my ignorance of the orders of your school makes it impossible for me to assign what time you should spend in private devotions, yet I'm sure if you do but really experience what it is to love God, you'll redeem all the time you can for his more immediate service. What is in your own power you may dispose of, nor are your rules so strict as not to admit of some diversions. I'll tell you what rule I used to observe when I was in my Father's house, and perhaps had as little, if not less, liberty than you have now. I used to allow my self as much time for recreation as I spent in private devotion. Not that I always spent so much, but so far I gave my self leave to go, but no further. So likewise in all things else, appoint so much time for sleep, eating, company, &c . . .[2]

Such passages as these suggest that Susanna was both an

[1] Stevenson, op. cit., p. 193.
[2] Headingley MSS, C f. 4f.

earnest and a strong-willed child, and also give some insight into the ethos of a Puritan home. It should not be assumed that 'The education of Puritan children' necessarily involved 'an over-serious and humourless upbringing'.[1] There was a tone of high seriousness, of course, in any Puritan home; but it was by no means incompatible with recreation and laughter. Susanna makes it clear that she was allowed games and amusements as a child, and she by no means forbade them to her children. There were certainly games at Epworth, including an innocent game of cards, though no 'loud talking or playing', and Hetty Wesley recalled the joys of family life in the rectory:

> Nay, to high heaven for greater gifts I bend:
> Health I've enjoyed, and I had once a friend!
> Our labour sweet, if labour it might seem,
> Allowed the sportive and instructive scene.
> Yet here no lewd or useless wit was found;
> We poised the wavering sail with ballast sound.
> Learning here placed her richer stores in view,
> Or, winged with love, the minutes gaily flew![2]

It is significant that when Susanna made the time she spent in prayer the limit of the time she spent in play, she did so of her own free choice. No doubt her home was conducive to such a choice, but *she* made it. It was an act of self-discipline, not a self-denying ordinance imposed from above. Sound learning, true religion, gaiety and wit, marked the home of her children at Epworth. There is no reason to believe that any of these elements were lacking as she grew up in her father's house in Bishopsgate.

Such then was the temper of Susanna's home, and it seems clear that her Puritan upbringing marked her for life. She was always, in a spiritual as well as physical sense, Dr Annesley's daughter. It might be countered, however, that

[1] R. A. Marchant, *The Puritans and the Church Courts in the Diocese of York, 1560–1642*, (1960), p. 115.

[2] From her poem, 'A Farewell to the World', printed by Clarke, *Wesley Family*, II, 307f.

all that has been said of the influence of her Puritan home must be drastically revised in the light of the step which Susanna took in 1682. In her thirteenth year, by her own account, she deliberately left Dissent to join the Church of England. Does not this decision represent a quite radical breach with her Puritan past? It would be foolish to deny that it marked a very real turning-point in her life, but it is an over-simplification to see it as a cancellation of all that her Puritan childhood meant to her. She was a precocious child, coming thirteen, and on the threshold of young womanhood. In many ways her character was already formed, and the fact that she then changed her denomination need not imply a repudiation of her previous spiritual development.

Susanna wrote down a carefully considered account of her reasons for becoming an Anglican, and was about to send it to her son, Samuel, when the rectory fire of 1709 destroyed all her papers. As she explained to Samuel, 'Because I was educated among the Dissenters, and there was somewhat remarkable in my leaving them at so early an age, not being full thirteen, I had drawn up an account of the whole transaction, under which head I had included the main of the Controversy between them and the Established Church, as far as they had come to my knowledge; and then followed the reasons that determined my judgement to the preference of the Church of England. I had fairly transcribed a great part of it, but you writing to me for some directions about receiving the Sacrament, I begun a short discourse on that head, intending to send all together: but before I could finish my design, the flames consumed that with all the rest of my writings.'[1] This document would have been of supreme interest for an understanding of Susanna's religious development, and it is tantalizing to have to guess at its contents.

[1] Headingley MSS, c. f. 9 (11 October 1709). The letter is printed with alterations in Clarke, *Wesley Family*, II, 33.

Why did she become an Anglican? Was it through disenchantment with Nonconformity, or because her mind was gripped by the attractiveness of the Anglican synthesis—its carefully ordered worship, its sense of Christian continuity, its studied moderation? It may well have been both. Certainly, Susanna must have been familiar from girlhood with the main issues which divided Dissent from the Church of England, for her father's home and meeting-house were the scene of frequent discussions among his Nonconformist colleagues.[1] When she decided to join the Church in 1683, the Great Ejection of 1662 was more than twenty years away, and must have seemed to this intelligent child rather a matter of old, unhappy, far-off things, and battles long ago. At any rate, it had all happened before she was born, and she could view it fairly dispassionately. She must have heard the rights and wrongs of conformity debated *ad nauseam*. She would hear, too, equally bitter debates which centred on the internal divisions of Nonconformity, ranged as it was under its Presbyterian, Baptist and Independent banners. Did the obsession with 1662 and the interminable wrangles which marked the dissidence of Dissent, incline her to give a long, thoughtful, sympathetic look at the alternative presented by the Established Church?

When she did look at the Anglicanism which was nearest to her, there was much in it to command her respect, and make her willing to inquire further. It so happened that at this period there were preaching in London pulpits several Anglican divines who combined marked ability with moderate views and a distinctly charitable and irenical attitude towards Dissenters. Some of them had themselves made the very transition from Puritanism to Anglicanism which Susanna was contemplating. Notable among them was John Sharp, who years later as Archbishop of York was to prove

[1] For the Latin disputations held in Dr Annesley's vestry, see John Stoughton, *History of Religion in England* (6 vols., 1881), V, 287.

so good a friend to both Susanna and her husband. Sharp's biographer describes the change after 1670, when, 'Moderate Anglican opinion definitely swung in their (i.e. the Nonconformists') favour, and, indeed, even angled for their support, on conditions. Of this latter school of thought Sharp was by no means the least conspicuous member. He himself had sprung from a family of strong Puritan traditions, and in his extreme youth had favoured the doctrine of predestination; his best friend Tillotson had had yet closer affinities with Nonconformity; and Baxter, one of Dissent's most venerated champions, was actually worshipping in his church.'[1] Sharp's mother-in-law was puritanically minded, and so great an admirer of Baxter that she would not agree to her daughter's marriage to Sharp until Baxter had given his approval to the match. In a sermon of 1674, Sharp pleaded for a policy of tolerance towards the Nonconformists, and in his writings sought to persuade them back into the fold of the Establishment.

Other able and moderate Anglican divines were then to be found in London, whose sermons Susanna may have heard at first hand or through the discussions of her father's ministerial friends. They combined learning and preaching ability in a formidable way, and tried by their studied moderation to win Dissenters back to the Church. Perhaps the most notable was John Tillotson, later Archbishop of Canterbury, under whose preaching Richard Baxter sat with such profit. He had been a Puritan, and a colleague of Dr Annesley in the Morning Exercise at Cripplegate. He had married Elizabeth French, a niece of Oliver Cromwell, and was responsible for a number of efforts to make concessions to the Nonconformists' point of view, and so comprehend them within the national Church. In the words of

[1] A. Tindal Hart, *The Life and Times of John Sharp Archbishop of York*, (1949), p. 86. Sharp was Rector of St Giles-in-the-Fields, 1675–81. For Baxter's worshipping in Anglican parish churches, as well as in Nonconformist gatherings, see *Reliquiae Baxterianae*, ed. Matthew Sylvester (1696), p. 437.

John Dove,[1] 'Hitherto the pulpit had been the stronghold of puritanism; under Tillotson it became a powerful agency for weaning men from puritan ideas.' Did his preaching help to win Susanna for the Church?

Another influential and moderate Anglican was Thomas Tenison, the Vicar of St Martin-in-the-Fields from 1680 to 1692. At St Paul's from 1678 to 1689, the Dean was Edward Stillingfleet, who twenty years before he came to St Paul's had published, in his *Irenicum* (1659), proposals for a union between Presbyterians and Episcopalians. In 1681, a year or two before Susanna joined the Church, he brought out his *The Unreasonableness of Separation*, in which he set out fresh terms for the comprehension of the Dissenters within the Church.[2] In the same year, William Beveridge, Vicar of St Peter's, Cornhill, preached a sermon in his new church rebuilt after the Great Fire, in which he 'tried to commend the Book of Common Prayer to its opponents in a spirit, on the whole, of sweet reasonableness'.[3] That spirit, from all that we know of Susanna, would have made a powerful appeal to her, and this background of moderate Anglican opinion, together with her father's tolerant and catholic disposition, make the step which she took in 1682 much more readily intelligible.[4]

What were the personal repercussions of Susanna's decision? How, in particular, did her father view the matter? Before trying to answer these questions, it is well to note that Susanna's account of her change suggests a studied modera-

[1] John Dove, *Biographical History of the Wesley Family*, (1840), p. 38. For his Puritan background, see T. Birch, *Life of Tillotson*, p. 5.

[2] For details, see C. E. Whiting, *Studies in English Puritanism from the Restoration to the Revolution, 1660–1688*, (1931), p. 526f.

[3] Whiting, op. cit., p. 531.

[4] For the spate of pamphlets put out by Anglican divines at this period and intended to deal with 'cases of conscience' raised by the scruples of Non-conformists over Anglican worship and teaching, see Whiting, *Studies in English Puritanism*, pp. 536–7. The whole of his long chapter on 'The theological controversy between Church and Dissent' in the period 1660–89, sheds considerable light on Susanna's decision.

tion, not an act of rebellion against her family and her upbringing. When she became an Anglican, she did not unchurch the Dissenters, but merely expressed her own considered 'preference of the Church of England'. Nonetheless, there were reasons why Dr Annesley should have felt very bitter about her return to the Church which had compelled him to renounce his living. He and his friends had suffered considerably for their Nonconformity, and at this very period (1682) his house was broken into by the informers and his goods distrained for breaches of the harsh religious laws against Nonconformists.[1] He had taken every care of his daughter's religious education, only to find that it had led her into the Conformist camp. A child's change of religious allegiance, even when the child is of mature years and the times are not torn by religious controversy, nearly always involves much heart-searching for the devout parent. *A fortiori*, then, to have a daughter go over to another communion before she had reached thirteen, and in the embittered religious atmosphere of the 1680s, might well have seemed to warrant Dr Annesley's putting his foot down, and forbidding his daughter to go any further in the matter until she was of age to judge for herself.

This might well have been the attitude of a Puritan father; it says a great deal for Dr Annesley that it was not his. He respected his young daughter's conscientious decision, and allowed it to make no difference in their personal relations. To the end of his life, Susanna remained his favourite daughter, and it was to her he bequeathed all his manuscripts and sermons.[2] On Susanna's side, her affection for her father was quite unabated. She named her first child Samuel, perhaps after her father as well as her husband, and one of the twins born in 1694 was called Annesley. When her father had been dead forty years, Susanna is found writing to her

[1] See above, p. 27.
[2] These too, unfortunately, were lost in the fire of 1709 at Epworth Rectory.

son, Charles, lamenting his brother Samuel's death, but comforting herself with some words of her father: 'As your good old grandfather often used to say, "That is an affliction, that God makes an affliction!"' [1] No doubt many such sayings brought back to Susanna the kindness and wisdom of her father, qualities that were never more impressively displayed than when his youngest daughter made her peace with the Church which had driven him into the wilderness.

Dr Annesley's magnanimity is to be explained chiefly in terms of his personal character and convictions. His charitable temper has already been illustrated, and he would no doubt have endorsed his daughter Elizabeth's judgement, 'that different Names do not make different Religions; but the Image of Christ is the same Lovely Thing, whether formed in a Church or in a Meeting.' [2] He had never been a party man, and singled out for praise the moderation of his friend and colleague Thomas Brand, who 'exercised towards the Conforming Clergy' a 'right Christian Temper'. [3] All we know of him suggests that Dr Annesley did the same, and that he would think no worse of his daughter for becoming an Anglican, because she did so simply and sincerely in obedience to her mind and conscience. Since her conscience had led her to renounce no fundamental of the faith, but only to change her churchmanship, what objection could her father make? Had he not taught her to be utterly loyal to a conscience illuminated by the Word of God? And had not some of his own close associates, from the same conscientious scruples, chosen the path of conformity in 1662? That year had been such a time of sifting and testing, that any moderate Puritan of the stamp of Annesley or Baxter must inevitably

[1] Cit. Kirk, *The Mother of the Wesleys*, p. 224f. In context, the saying seems to mean that our relation to God determines whether or not a happening 'afflicts' or harms us. Prosperity may gravely harm a worldling, whereas, by God's grace, the believer may find that even sorrow yields a blessing.

[2] Rogers, *Character of a Good Woman*, p. 132f.

[3] Annesley, *Life and Funeral Sermon of the Reverend Mr Thomas Brand*, p.

have been torn between conformity and nonconformity. Dr Annesley could, therefore, well understand and sympathize with his daughter both in her dilemma and in her choice.

It is indeed a serious mistake to see 1662 as creating a complete rupture between the conforming and the nonconforming Puritans. Richard Baxter could write, some years after the Great Ejection, 'I still profess, that in all my experience, those called Nonconformists, did heartily love, honour, praise and hear a Bishop or Conformist that preached and lived seriously, spiritually, and in Christian Love, such as through God's mercy we have had many . . .'[1] Ralph Thoresby describes an impressive funeral of a leading Puritan divine, at which he saw more ministers together than on any previous occasion of his life. They followed the coffin two by two, a conformist and a nonconformist together, as a demonstration of their solidarity in mourning their brother. The Puritans of 1662 did not all make the same choice, but among the moderates on either side there was no final breach of fellowship, and the same was true of Susanna and her father when they found themselves on opposite sides of the Anglican-Nonconformist division after 1682. Susanna's continuing fellowship with her father, and the retention of her Puritan heritage, were to be vital factors in influencing her own household when she began to bring up her children in the faith of their fathers. The Annesley tradition was not lost upon the little Wesleys, and in one parsonage at least it was to prove true that if one scratched an Anglican, one would find a Puritan.

---

[1] Baxter, *An Apology for the Nonconformists' Ministry*, (1681), Preface. The work was mainly written in 1668-9.

CHAPTER THREE

Wife to Mr Wesley

> She was such a helpmate as Mr Wesley required; and
> to her, under God, the great eminence of the subse-
> quent Wesley family is to be attributed. *Adam Clarke*

IN 1682, at the wedding of her sister Elizabeth to
John Dunton, Susanna Annesley appears to have met for
the first time the man who was to be her husband. She was
then a girl of twelve, and Samuel Wesley a poor theological
student in training for the Dissenting Ministry at Mr Veal's
Academy. Samuel's poetic talents were made to serve the
occasion, and at the reception in Dr Annesley's house he
presented Dunton and his bride with an Epithalamium.[1] It
was no doubt very much a Nonconformist occasion, and yet
young Wesley may not have been entirely at his ease in the
gathering. He was ostensibly preparing for the Nonconformist

---

[1] Dunton, *Life and Errors*, I, 78, describes Wesley as an 'ingenious Gentleman'
and 'a Student in the Rev. Mr Veal's house'. For the identification of the poet
as Wesley, see Clarke, *Wesley Family*, I, 88, 118f. For Edward Veal, see *D.N.B.*
and A. G. Matthews, *Calamy Revised*, (1934), s.v. Veal.

Ministry, but his studies of the controversy between Dissent and the Establishment were beginning to draw him towards the Anglican position. He described later how the crude political and religious extremism of some of his fellow-students helped to confirm him in his trend of thought away from Dissent.[1] At the same time Susanna, bred up in the atmosphere of theological debate, was being led by her reading in a similar direction. Love and theological accord ripened together. Samuel was able to steer Susanna away from the Socinian heresy, which for a time, in her search for her own religious position, she had entertained. Within a year or two of their first meeting, Samuel exchanged Stoke Newington Dissenting Academy[2] for Exeter College, Oxford, having walked down to the University with only forty-five shillings in his pocket, and paid his first caution money in the September of 1684.[3] By 1688, when he had proceeded B.A. and been ordained deacon with a curacy of £28 a year, they were able to contemplate marriage. After being ordained priest (24 February 1689), Samuel served for a time as a naval chaplain, with a handsome stipend of £70. He then resigned the service, returned to civilian life and a lower income, and on the strength of a London curacy of £30 a year, married Susanna.[4]

Susanna's choice of a husband presented her father with another test of character and of grace. She had not only turned Anglican, but had now married a strong High-Churchman and lapsed Dissenter. Whatever Dr Annesley's feelings may have been, there was no discernible sign of resentment on his part against the young couple. Adam

[1] For examples of extremist opinion among Dissenters, see Whiting, *Studies in English Puritanism*, p. 464.
[2] He had removed to Stoke Newington, where Mr Charles Morton had an Academy, when Mr Veal's establishment closed down.
[3] Clarke, *Wesley Family*, I, 99, 236.
[4] The marriage date is uncertain. Clarke, op. cit., II, 2, puts it 'about the year 1689', though earlier (I, 183) he says Samuel had only 'contracted an acquaintance' with Susanna 'about 1690 or 1691'.

Clarke made his own inquiries on the point from a surviving member of the Wesley family, a granddaughter of Samuel, who assured him: 'I do not find that Dr Annesley or any of his family were prejudiced against my grandfather for leaving the dissenters; but his mind was too enlarged to be prejudiced, whatever preference he had to his own community.'[1] Dr Annesley's own 'preference' (as opposed to 'prejudice'), was Presbyterian; but as he had acquiesced in his young daughter's 'preference of the Church of England',[2] so he now accepted her husband's, which had led him not only into the Church of England, but into her ministry. Fortunately for the bridegroom, his swingeing attack on the Dissenters and their academies, though already committed to paper at the time of his marriage, was not published until some years later. When Wesley's *A Letter from a Country Divine . . . Concerning the Education of the Dissenters in their Private Academies* came off the press in 1703, Dr Annesley had been dead for half a dozen years. Otherwise, for all his tolerance and charity, Susanna's father might have been hard put to give his consent and blessing to the match. He would certainly have hesitated had he been able to look ahead for half a century and listen to Samuel Wesley indulging in a bout of self-congratulation at having instilled High Church principles into all his children. His grandchildren, Dr Annesley would have learned, had been imbued with 'a steady opposition and confederacy against all such as are avowed and declared enemies to God and his clergy; and who deny or disbelieve any articles of natural or revealed religion; as well as to such as are open or secret friends to the Great Rebellion; or to any such principles as do but squint towards the same practices; so that he hopes they are all staunch high church, and for inviolable passive obedience; from which if any of them should be so wicked as to

---

[1] Clarke, *Wesley Family*, II, 2.
[2] So Susanna herself described it; see above, p. 57.

degenerate, he can't tell whether he could prevail with himself to give them his blessing'.[1]

Soon after their marriage, Samuel secured, through the good offices of his friend and benefactor, the Marquis of Normanby, the rectory of South Ormsby in the Lincolnshire Wolds.[2] So, in 1690, Susanna left the busy capital where she had spent her girlhood for the provincial backwater of eighteenth-century Lincolnshire. She was not to see London again until 1724, when she made her abortive journey to meet her brother on his return from India.[3] It was a drastic rustication, for the isolation and insularity of Lincolnshire were proverbial. Geography had of course a good deal to do with its insularity, and Sir Francis Hill has well described the physical features which severed the county from the rest of the country. To the east, the sea; to the north, the Humber; to the west the Trent; and, 'Even when it was not in flood the Trent was a physical and psychological barrier. It had no bridge below Newark until Gainsborough bridge was built in 1790. There were only ferries, as at Gainsborough, Dunham, Littleborough and Stockwith. No main roads led to them. The county of Lincoln was virtually a peninsula, whose neck to the south was narrowed by the fens.'[4] A century and a half earlier, Henry VIII had dubbed the county, 'one of the most brute and beastly of the whole realm,' and though the king was biased, there was truth in his verdict. The Wesleys were to find it still true in 1690, in the remoter parts of the county at least, and especially after they moved to Epworth, where there was brutality and beastliness in plenty.

For the moment, however, the future for Mr and Mrs Wesley seemed tolerably bright. They brought with them

---

[1] Clarke, *Wesley Family*, II, 234f.
[2] The patrons of the living were the Massingberd family. See L. Tyerman, *The Life and Times of the Rev. Samuel Wesley, M.A.* (1866), p. 467.
[3] See above, p. 44.
[4] J. W. F. Hill, *Tudor and Stuart Lincoln*, (1956), p. 1.

to South Ormsby their first child, they were free of debt, and Samuel's living had a nominal value of £50 a year. The long struggle against poverty and ill-health, which was to tax all Susanna's heroic resources of body and spirit, still lay in the future. As they started their new life together, the country parson and his wife had a great deal to bind them together besides their mutual love. They had a shared background as lapsed Dissenters, uncommon courage and tenacity of purpose, and a real concern for Christianity in earnest. Yet there were inevitable tensions between two such strong and contrasted personalities. Though Susanna's heart and soul were in the heavenly places, her feet were planted firmly on the earth. She was able to combine, in a quite astonishing way, a firm grasp of all the multifarious activities of a large household, with something of the disciplined devotion of the monastic life. Her husband, on the other hand, lived half his life in a scholarly world of his own, absorbed in his writings, and hopelessly impractical in money matters. Samuel knew his own defect, and when the end of 1700 found him £300 in debt, he acknowledged that his own incapacity was partly to blame. By this date he had been at Epworth for three years, but he had not yet recovered from the expenses of his seven years at South Ormsby. He wrote a plaintive letter to his benefactor, John Sharp, Archbishop of York, setting out the stages which had led to his parlous financial position: ' 'Twill be no great wonder that when I had but fifty pounds per annum for six or seven years together, nothing to begin the world with, one child at least per annum, and my wife sick for half that time, that I should run one hundred and fifty pounds behind hand; especially when about a hundred of it had been expended in goods, without doors and within.' Yet he had the honesty to admit, 'I doubt not but one reason of my being sunk so far is, my not understanding worldly affairs.'[1]

[1] Clarke, *Wesley Family*, I, 191.

Samuel was at the time of writing thirty-four years old, but when he was over seventy and trying, with only moderate success, to rebut the charge of feckless extravagance which his own brother had brought against him, he had resort to the same excuse. Writing in the third person, as if to emphasize that he was taking a completely detached view of himself, he replied to Matthew Wesley: 'As for his folly, he owns he can hardly demur to the charge; for he fairly acknowledges he never was, nor ever will be, like the children of this world, who are accounted wise in their generation, in doting upon this world, courting this world, and regarding nothing else: not but that he has all his life laboured truly both with his hands, head, and heart, to provide things honest in the sight of all men . . .'[1] No one knew his weakness better than Susanna. Her brother Samuel, the East India merchant, had prevailed on her husband to act as his agent for some business dealings in England. The business apparently failed through Wesley's neglect and incompetence, and Annesley quarrelled with his brother-in-law over the matter. Some years after the breach, Susanna wrote a reasoned letter to her brother, defending her husband from his charges, and saying in effect, that he should have known better than to give Wesley such a commission. To Annesley's charge that Wesley 'is not fit for wordly business', Susanna can, however, do nothing but agree: 'This I likewise assent to, and must own I was mistaken when I did think him fit for it: my own experience hath since convinced me that he is one of those who, our Saviour saith, "are not so wise in their generation as the children of this world".'[2] There was no question of Samuel's honesty and integrity, but he had no head for business. His wife, so eminently practical and competent herself, must have found it peculiarly galling to see him floundering in his management of the family's affairs. He

[1] Clarke, *Wesley Family*, I, 235.
[2] Ibid., I, 392.

would assuredly have spent more than the few months of 1705 in a debtor's prison if he had not had in Susanna such a helpmate as his needs required.

A further contrast in personality between Susanna and Samuel lay in what the Middle Ages would have called the prevailing 'humour' of their characters. Susanna, though an extremely strong personality, was quiet, restrained, modest, self-possessed. In Samuel, on the other hand, there was not only a choleric temper, but a streak of personal vanity, a tendency to strike a pose and act a part. Here, no doubt, Susanna's Puritan training had merely reinforced her natural bent; but the same training had not sufficed to purge her husband of his love of self-display. This strain in Samuel comes out in his literary ambitions, his readiness to cast himself in the role of writer and poet. The title of his first published work, written in 1685 while he was an under-graduate at Oxford, sets the tone. It was a collection of, 'Poems on Several Subjects never before Handled', which he entitled simply, *Maggots*, a seventeenth century use of the word which can perhaps be best rendered by the modern 'whimsies'. As a man might have a bee in his bonnet, so he might have a maggot in his mind, and Samuel duly showed himself, in the frontispiece of the work, with a maggot curling up from his poetic brow and seeking an outlet in print.

His first printed book consisted of poems, and it was as a poet that he loved to figure himself. Writing to the Arch-bishop of York in 1702, in the midst of debts and difficulties, he could say of himself and his poverty, 'He that's born to be a poet must, I am afraid, live and die so.'[1] He is probably only half-serious here, but his words are still significant, especially when taken with those of an earlier letter, where in all gravity he thanks the Archbishop for his generosity and adds: 'Certainly, never did an archbishop of England write in such a manner to an isle-poet: but it is peculiar to your

[1] Clarke, *Wesley Family*, I, 206.

Grace to oblige so as none besides can do it.'[1] It is typical
of Samuel that even in the midst of acute poverty, he is not
simply a poor country clergyman, but an 'isle-poet'; and
even though the isle is not Lyonnesse or Innisfree, but only
Axholme, the title carries with it an aura of romance which
helps to alleviate his condition. His brother-in-law, John
Dunton, reflected on the sales of books of poems he had
published, and commented wryly, 'It is something un-
accountable, but one would incline to think there is some
indispensable Law, whereby Poverty and Disappointment
are entailed upon Poets.'[2] Samuel Wesley accepted the entail
as an essential part of a poet's estate.

It need hardly be said that Samuel was emphatically not
a great poet, though he had some excuse for thinking himself
one. Had not Nahum Tate, the Poet Laureate, extolled
Samuel's long poem on the *Life of Christ*, in his preface to
the 1697 edition? Samuel's self-esteem had feasted itself upon
Tate's opening lines:

> As when some prophet, who had long retir'd,
> Returns from solitude with rapture fired . . .
> So you, great bard, who lay till now concealed,
> Compiling what your heavenly muse revealed,
> No sooner quit the shade, but strike our eyes
> With wonder, and our minds with ecstacies.[3]

The rector's son, Samuel, had been more guarded in his
praise of this work, acknowledging merely that, 'Whate'er
his strains, still glorious was his end'; and to do him justice
the author's own estimate of his achievement was a distinctly
modest one: 'The cuts are good, the notes pretty good, the
verses so so.'[4] In short, despite Adam Clarke's strange
judgement on Wesley's poem *Eupolis' Hymn to the Creator*—

---

[1] Clarke, *Wesley Family*, I, 197.
[2] Dunton, *Life and Errors*, I, 183.
[3] Clarke, *Wesley Family*, I, 136.
[4] Clarke, *Wesley Family*, I, 139.

'a piece of exquisite merit', and 'the finest in the English language'[1]—there is little doubt that John Dunton made a much more realistic appraisal of his brother-in-law's poetic talents: 'Mr Wesley had an early inclination to Poetry, but he usually wrote too fast to write well. Two hundred couplets a day are too many by two-thirds to be well-furnished with all the beauties and the graces of that art. He wrote very much for me both in Verse and Prose, though I shall not name over the titles, in regard I am altogether as unwilling to see my name at the bottom of them, as Mr Wesley would be to subscribe his own.'[2] Before Dunton wrote these words, he and Wesley had quarrelled, but the publisher could still give a reasonably charitable estimate of his author's character. Though Dunton and Wesley fell apart, they had a good deal in common, and notably a love of being in the public eye, a flair for publicity, and a more than average dash of personal vanity. It was not only his fervent royalism which led Samuel to dedicate so many of his writings to members of the royal family; it was also an eye to the main chance and to the impressiveness of the title-page. Again, it was not simply devotion to duty and loyal support of the Church, though these motives had their place, which led him to shoulder the burden of acting as a Proctor in Convocation for the Diocese of Lincoln. His three-year term of service cost him £150 in expenses, money which he and his family could ill afford. Yet for Samuel there were real compensations. The work would take him to London for several months of the year, and open to him the literary world of the capital again. It would give him a chance to play some part in the councils of the Church, and might open to him the road of preferment. Yet preferment or no preferment, the mere opportunity to be at the centre of ecclesiastical affairs would

---

[1] Ibid. (1823 edn.), pp. 129, 149. In the 1836 edition, Clarke moderates his praise, and calls the poem, 'the finest on the subject in the English language' (I, 231).

[2] Dunton, *Life and Errors*, I, 164.

be reward enough to a man of Samuel's temperament. He would, moreover, have been less than human if he had not welcomed Convocation as a heaven-sent opportunity to get away from the fens of Epworth, from his crude and brutal parishioners, his unending debts, and his houseful of children. His optimism was of the Micawber calibre, and no doubt it did not take him long to shed his cares as he rode down to London. Despite the £50 expense sheet, 'It was a glorious thing to be a Convocation man.'

This same side of Samuel's nature, his desire to cut a public figure and his highly-developed sense of his own importance, appears again in the list of his patrons and benefactors he sent to Archbishop Sharp in 1703. He might be a miserable debtor, the list implies, but at least he could bask in the reflected glory of having been assisted by the highest in the land. The names roll from his pen as if taken from a Court Circular: the Marchioness of Normanby, the Lady Northampton, the Duke and Duchess of Buckingham, the Queen (the names are not in order of precedence!), the Bishop of Salisbury, and the Archbishop of York.[1] It was almost worth being in debt to be able to claim affinity with all these notabilities. The same trait in Samuel's character appears even in small details, so that when he wished to illustrate his great folio commentary on *Job* with an engraving of a war-horse, nothing would content him but he must write to Lord Oxford, asking permission to reproduce a picture of, 'the finest Arab horse in the world', namely his lordship's 'Bloody Arab'.[2] His lordship was naturally only too ready to grant so innocent and flattering a request. John Wesley's story of his father's having written Dr Henry Sacheverell's speech at his impeachment for his High Church political pronouncements in 1709, is of the same ilk. It may be an exaggeration, but it is utterly in character, for Samuel

[1] Clarke, *Wesley Family*, II, 210.
[2] Clarke, *Wesley Family*, I, 245.

could never resist a fight, and always revelled in being at the
centre of affairs.

Yet if Samuel liked to see himself in the roles of poet,
literary figure, leading churchman, and man of affairs, it
was not sheer personal vanity which prompted his aspira-
tions. He was a man of real abilities, and might legitimately
have expected to play a larger part in the life of the Church
than he was able to do as rector of Epworth. Certainly he was
capable of doing so, for he had the scholarly equipment, the
integrity of character, and the pastoral and evangelical
concern, which might have fitted him for a bishop. It is
likely, then, that there was a genuine element of frustration
and of inability to find full scope for his gifts, in his desire
to escape from Epworth into a wider world. His patron, the
Marquis of Normanby, did in fact try to secure his presentation to an Irish bishopric when the sees of Ross and Cloyne
fell vacant just before Wesley was appointed to Epworth.
The Marquis wrote to Archbishop Tillotson, himself a
former Puritan associate of Susanna's father, urging Wesley's
claims, but when the Archbishop consulted King William,
'His Majesty,' in Tillotson's words, 'according to his true
judgement did by no means think fit.' It was this episode
which led John Dunton to characterize his brother-in-law,
the erstwhile Dissenter and would-be Bishop, as, 'Sam.
Wesley, who fouled his nest in hopes of a bishopric.' It was
a racy, but uncharitable epigram, for Samuel Wesley had too
much courage and integrity ever to be a mere place-seeker.
Moreover, Susanna herself thought that his gifts were wasted
at Epworth, though she did not put it quite so baldly. In one
of her rare moments of repining, she exclaimed in a letter to
her brother, Samuel Annesley, 'Did I not know that Almighty
Wisdom hath views and ends, in fixing the bounds of our
habitation, which are out of our ken, I should think it a
thousand pities that a man of his brightness, and rare
endowments of learning and useful knowledge, in relation to

75

the church of God, should be confined to an obscure corner of the country, where his talents are buried, and he determined to a way of life for which he is not so well qualified as I could wish . . .' Susanna penned those words, in 1722, with much feeling, for by then she and Samuel had been 'confined to an obscure corner of the country' for a quarter of a century, and had slight prospect of any release.[1]

Samuel's genuine theological learning found an early outlet in the pages of the *Athenian Mercury*, a periodical which from 1691 he edited jointly with John Dunton and Richard Sault, assisted by 'the ingenious Dr Norris'.[2] They undertook to answer questions relating to any branch of literature— historical, scientific, theological, philosophical . . . —and succeeded in gathering together a distinguished band of contributors, including Daniel Defoe, Jonathan Swift, and Sir William Temple. In the advertisement for the eighteenth volume of the periodical, the editors promised, with all the rash confidence of youth, to answer, 'all the most nice and curious questions proposed by Ladies and Gentlemen, relating to Divinity, Philosophy, Love, Marriage, History, Physick, Law, Mathematicks and Trade, &c.' Predictably, the most popular branches of knowledge seem to have been Love and Marriage, and a fair proportion of the queries submitted in the early numbers were of the kind which still form the staple of the letters to the women's magazines. Question 4 of the issue of Tuesday, September 5th 1693, is a typical sample of the *genre*: 'A Friend of mine having a Kindness for a young Gentlewoman, and hath by keeping of her Company from time to time, so entangled himself . . .' etc., etc.[3] The versatile editors were fully alive to the need for

---

[1] For the low condition, both material and intellectual, of many of the country clergy in the late seventeenth century, when Wesley first came to Lincolnshire, see John Eachard, *The Grounds and Occasions of the Contempt of the Clergy*, (1670).

[2] Dunton, *Life and Errors*, I, 189f.

[3] *Athenian Mercury*, II, no. 17.

'human interest', but neither that nor the genuine learning which adorned its pages could keep the paper in being for much more than a few years. When the *Mercury* ceased publication, Swift wrote a long and enthusiastic ode in praise of the three anonymous editors, and regretted its disappearance:

> I grieve this noble work, so happily begun,
> So quickly and so wonderfully carried on,
> Must fall at last to interest, folly, and abuse.[1]

Wesley's responsibility was to deal with questions on poetry, theology, and church history. Almost forty years after the episode of the short-lived *Mercury*, Swift was to have the merits of Wesley's theological scholarship brought to his attention once more, in a letter from the poet Pope, canvassing support for Samuel's commentary on *Job*:

This is a letter extraordinary, to do and to say nothing, but to recommend to you (as a clergyman and a charitable one) a pious and a good work, and for a good and honest man. Moreover, he is about seventy, and poor, which you might think included in the word honest. I shall think it a kindness done to myself if you can propagate Mr Wesley's subscription for his "Commentary on Job" among your divines (bishops excepted, of whom there is no hope), and among such as are believers or readers of the Scriptures. Even the curious may find something to please them, if they scorn to be edified. It has been the labour of eight years of this learned man's life: I call him what he is, a learned man; and I engage you will approve his prose more than you formerly did his poetry. Lord Bolingbroke is a favourer of it, and allows you to do your best to serve an old Tory, and a sufferer for the Church of England, though you are a Whig, as I am.[2]

Pope was right; Samuel was indeed 'a learned man'. Yet Susanna had married a man who had more than scholarship to his credit, for her husband was possessed of genuine piety and a real pastoral concern. A contemporary character sketch, by Charles Gildon, who had worked with Wesley on

[1] Clarke, *Wesley Family*, I, 126.
[2] Clarke, *Wesley Family*, I, 138. Letter dated April 12th, 1730.

the *Athenian Mercury*, sets his learning in the context of his spiritual gifts, and suggests part of the attraction he must have had for the devout and earnest young Susanna:

He was a man of profound knowledge, not only of the Holy Scriptures, of the councils, and of the Fathers, but also of every other art that comes within those called liberal. His zeal and ability in giving spiritual directions were great. With invincible power he confirmed the wavering, and confuted heretics. Beneath the genial warmth of his wit the most barren subject became fertile and divertive. His style was sweet and manly, soft without satiety, and learned without pedantry. His temper and conversation were affable. His compassion for the sufferings of his fellow-creatures was as great as his learning and his parts. Were it possible for any man to act the part of a universal priest, he would certainly deem it his duty to take care of the spiritual good of all mankind. In all his writings and actions he evinced a deep concern for all that bear the glorious image of their Maker, and was so apostolical in his spirit, that pains, labours, watchings, and prayers were far more delightful to him than honours to the ambitious, wealth to the miser, or pleasure to the voluptuous.[1]

It is an impressive picture, and is corroborated by the evidence of his life. It is also striking in that it might equally well have been written of his son John, with barely a word altered. The skill in spiritual direction, the wit, the manly style, the compassion for the poor,—all these John Wesley shared to the full. The 'part of a universal priest' might well be assigned to John, who looked upon the whole world as his parish, and whose letters to men and women all over the British Isles are full of pastoral counsel and concern. The 'apostolical spirit' of the father bore fruit in the ceaseless missionary labours of the son.

Samuel's compassion and universal humanity were seen in his undergraduate days, when he visited the Oxford prisons, as John and Charles were to do in their turn, as members of the Holy Club.[2] An incident which sharply focuses Samuel's generosity, however, has come to light

---

[1] Cit. Stevenson, *Memorials of the Wesley Family*, pp. 63–4.
[2] Clarke, *Wesley Family*, I, 100.

only as recently as 1963. The evidence comes, appropriately, from Oxford itself. Two manuscript copies of letters written by Samuel Wesley in 1692 and 1698, discovered in the Bodleian Library by Miss H. A. Beecham of Nottingham University, have disclosed some new and interesting details of his early life. Samuel describes in the 1692 letter how desperately poor he had become at the end of his first three months in Oxford, when he found himself, 'somdays getting Meat & others none, all my stock in ye world being only one 8 farthings.' He goes on to tell how,

. . . when I was in the midst of theise Extremitys, wch were rendered sharper by ye season of ye year, it being ye height of winter & a very severe one, I walkt out in the morning alone, behind ye New Parks, & as I went musing along in an unfrequented path near ye Rivers side I saw a little Boy about som seaven or 8 years old, lying under a Hedg and crying bitterly I went up to him & askt him ye reason, He told me y^t two days before his Father died, His Mother having bin dead severall years, & left none in ye House but himself & a little sister about ten years old, without any victualls or money that they had stayd at home all the next day but none took care of them nor brought them any releif That they resolv'd in ye morning, she should go a begging in their own Parish, about a mile or two from Oxford and he would go to ye City & try what they could get to keep themselves alive, accordingly he told Me he gott up as soon as 'twas day, & walkt toward Oxford, but being weak through a long ague & want of meat, was forc'd to lie down there & could go No further; I confess I was toucht wth ye poor Boys story, I rais'd him from ye ground to wch his cloaths were almost frozen, & rubb'd his limbs, benum'd & almost dead with the cold, till he could Make a shift to go, then I pulld out my 2^d, all ye stock I had in the world, & gave it him, seeing him in greater extremity than I was myself, wth wch he went overjoyd into ye town, & bought a twopenny loaf wch he carryd home to his sister . . .[1]

Samuel's concern for the poor took in their spiritual needs as well, and when he was imprisoned for debt in Lincoln Castle during three months of 1705, he quickly bestirred

[1] H. A. Beecham, Samuel Wesley Senior: New Biographical Evidence (*Renaissance and Modern Studies*, VII, 1963), p. 104f.

himself in a pastoral ministry to his fellow-prisoners. He wrote quite cheerfully from his debtor's prison to the Archbishop of York:

I don't despair of doing some good here (and so long I sha'n't quite lose the end of living), and it may be, do more in this new parish than in my old one; for I have leave to read prayers every morning and afternoon here in the prison, and to preach once a Sunday, which I choose to do in the afternoon, when there is no sermon at the minster. And I'm getting acquainted with my brother jail-birds as fast as I can; and shall write to London next post, to the Society for propagating Christian Knowledge, who, I hope, will send me some books to distribute among them.[1]

Archbishop Sharp might well have been proud to have such a clergyman in his province. This strain of true religion in the man emerged strongly at his end, when he expressed to his two sons his deepest convictions about the Faith. 'The inward witness, son, the inward witness,' he told John, 'that is the proof, the strongest proof, of Christianity.' As he laid his hands on Charles's head, he spoke in prophetic terms of a revival of Christianity in England: 'Be steady. The Christian faith will surely revive in this kingdom; you shall see it, though I shall not.'[2] Samuel Wesley was not only a man of learning, but a man of faith, and John Dunton, though strongly critical of his brother-in-law, spoke no less than the truth in his final assessment of him: 'I could be very maggoty in the Character of this Conforming Dissenter ... but, except he further provokes me, I bid him Farewell till we meet in Heaven; and there I hope we shall renew our friendship, for, human frailties excepted, I believe Sam Wesley a pious man.'[3] There is little doubt that Susanna, though she had to make far greater allowance for her husband's 'human frailties', believed so too.

[1] Clarke, *Wesley Family*, I, 214.
[2] Clarke, *Wesley Family*, I, 344ff.
[3] Dunton, *Life and Errors*, I, 164f.

The more attractive side of Samuel's character was not confined to his genuine piety and good works. There was about him also a warmth of feeling, a zest for life, a real humanity, and a strong sense of humour. A number of his choicer quips and comments have come down to us. He was amused at his young son John's careful and logical approach to life, and remarked to Susanna, that he did not believe the child would attend to the most pressing needs of nature, unless he could give a reason for it! When the ghost, or poltergeist, 'Old Jeffrey', disturbed the Epworth household in 1716–17, the rector reflected that the story of the events, 'would make a glorious penny book for Jack Dunton!'[1] He was not above playing a crude prank on his parish clerk,[2] and his exuberant outburst when John was elected to a fellowship of Lincoln College, is well known. Shrugging aside momentarily all his debts and troubles, he dilated with pride at his son's distinction, and wrote enthusiastically to the new Fellow, 'Wherever I am, my Jack is Fellow of Lincoln!'[3] His resilience, his capacity to rise above his domestic worries and the treadmill of debt repayment, never left him. A short letter to the Archbishop of York, written from Epworth on 18th May 1701, is typical of his hearty cheerfulness in the face of domestic trials:

My Lord,
This comes as a rider to the last, by the same post, to bring such news as I presume will not be unwelcome to a person who has so particular a concern for me. Last night my wife brought me a *few* children. There are but *two* yet, a boy and a girl, and I think they are all at present: we have had four in two years and a day, three of which are living.

Never came any thing more like a gift from heaven than what the Countess of Northampton sent by your Lordship's charitable offices. Wednesday evening my wife and I clubbed and joined stocks, which came but to *six shillings*, to send for coals. Thursday

---

[1] Clarke, *Wesley Family*, I, 269.
[2] Ibid., I, 357f.
[3] Ibid., I, 306.

morning I received the *ten pounds*; and at night my wife was delivered. Glory be to God for His unspeakable goodness!

I am

Your Grace's most obliged

and most humble servant

S. WESLEY.[1]

Susanna was married to a man of spirit, who had the capacity to laugh at himself, and so surmount his troubles; but a man too who had the sterner virtue of courage. His career is punctuated with examples of it. As a young clergyman, he heard an army officer swearing obscenely in a London coffee-house, and sent the waiter over with a glass of water to wash the foulness from his mouth,—a challenge which would have led to a *fracas* if the man's friends had not restrained him. He dealt firmly with his patron's mistress when he found her passing the time of day with his young wife, even though his action lost him the living of South Ormsby. John Wesley records the incident:

My father's first preferment in the church was a small parish (South Ormsby) obtained for him by the Marquis of Normanby. This nobleman had a house in the parish, where a woman who lived with him usually resided. This lady *would* be intimate with my mother, whether *she* would or not. To such an intercourse my father would not submit. Coming in one day, and finding this obtrusive visitant sitting with my mother, he went up to her, took her by the hand, and very fairly handed her out. The nobleman resented the affront so outrageously as to make it necessary for my father to resign the living.[2]

He knew too how to stand up to the threats and brutality of the Epworth roughs, when his outspoken preaching or his unpopular political convictions caused him to fall foul of them. They slashed his cows, burned his crops, and menaced his family and his person, but it took more than all that to

[1] Clarke, *Wesley Family*, I, 198.

[2] Clarke, *Wesley Family*, I, 107f., and see I, 204f. The nobleman was not in fact the Marquis of Normanby, who continued to use his influence on Samuel Wesley's behalf, but a member of the local Massingberd family. See L. Tyerman, *The Life and Times of the Rev. Samuel Wesley*, p. 467.

make so stubborn a man as Wesley yield. He wrote to the Archbishop of York from Lincoln Castle, where his enemies had had him lodged for debt,

Most of my friends advise me to leave Epworth if e'er I should get from hence. I confess I am not of that mind, because I may yet do good there; and 'tis like a coward, to desert my post because the enemy fire thick upon me. They have only wounded me yet, and I believe CAN'T kill me. I hope to be at home by Xmass. God help my poor family! . . .[1]

There was no doubt of Samuel's moral courage, and on an issue of principle he would not budge. As a young man he had refused to read James II's Declaration of Indulgence, because it was intended to advance the interests of the Roman Catholics. He would not read it, 'though strongly solicited by some of the King's friends to do it; and he not only refused to read the Declaration, but, though surrounded with *courtiers*, *soldiers* and *informers*, preached a bold Discourse pointedly against it, from Dan. iii. 17, 18.'[2]

Such tenacious holding to principle was admirable, but Samuel had the defects of his virtues. He was not only brave and high-principled, he was also hot-tempered and stubborn to a degree. He contended fiercely for points of moral substance, but also for his own preferences and prejudices. He had Irish blood in him, and there was more than a little of the fighting Irishman in his composition. Quick-tempered and quarrelsome, he managed at one time or another to cross most of his friends and associates: John Dunton, the Dissenters, his Epworth parishioners, his brother-in-law Samuel Annesley, John Whitelamb, his amanuensis, and, of course, his wife, Susanna. His differences with Susanna throw a great deal of light on their temperaments and on their relationship as man and wife. How did two such strong and contrasted characters manage to live together for so long in reasonable harmony? Samuel's own version of their life

[1] Clarke, *Wesley Family*, I, 218. The letter is dated 12 September 1705.
[2] Clarke, *Wesley Family* (1823 edn.), p. 156f.

together was contained in his poem, the *Life of Christ*, in which, within a few years of their marriage, he reviewed in complacent couplets his apparently ideal relationship with his young wife:

> She graced my humble roof, and blest my life,
> Blest me by a far greater name than wife;
> Yet still I bore an undisputed sway,
> Nor was't her task, but pleasure to obey;
> Scarce thought, much less could act, what I denied,
> In our low house, there was no room for pride;
> Nor need I e'er direct what still was right,
> Still [*sic*] studied my convenience and delight . . .[1]

The unconscious irony of the line, 'In our low house there was no room for pride', is astonishing when it is remembered what a fierce, proud, intolerant little man the rector of Epworth was. When all allowance has been made for poetic licence, it is very difficult to accept this description as an objective account of their married life. For Susanna's side of the story, and a much more credible picture, we may turn to a letter of 1725, in which she confesses to her son John, "Tis an unhappiness almost peculiar to our family, that your father and I seldom think alike'.[2] The impression that the domestic harmony was not quite so perfect as the poetic husband suggests, is confirmed by Samuel Wesley the younger, who in a letter to John includes a passing reference to their parents: 'My wife and I join in love and duty, and beg my father's and mother's blessing. I would to God they were as easy in one another, and as little uneasy in their fortunes, as we are!'[3] Both these letters were written after Samuel and Susanna had been married for thirty-five years or more, but the evidence suggests that the tension they describe was of long standing.

[1] Samuel Wesley, *The Life of our Blessed Lord & Saviour Jesus Christ*, (1693), p. 40.

[2] Ms. Letter, Wesley's Chapel, City Road, E.C.1.; Printed in full in *Wesley's Chapel Magazine*, Jan. 1965.

[3] Clarke, *Wesley Family*, II, 166. Letter dated 18 November 1727.

The signs of friction which *a priori* we should expect from their temperamental differences, are certainly discernible. How, then, was domestic peace preserved? By outward submission, no doubt, on Susanna's part, for whether or not it was her 'pleasure', she did learn to 'obey', addressing her husband as 'Sir' and referring to him as 'My Master' throughout her married life. At the same time, feminine tact would give her, unobtrusively but no less really, a good deal of her own way. Whether or not Samuel ever became to Susanna, in Mrs Harrison's rather too colourful phrase, no more than, 'the hair-shirt of her cloister',[1] she learned how to manage him, and to deal with him as one difficulty among many. There was, moreover, in the natural division of labour between the rector and his wife, a factor conducive to domestic harmony. Each had his or her own sphere, and while they kept within these, friction was unlikely to be serious. His was the church, the parish, the study; hers, the kitchen, the nursery, the classroom; and each resented intrusion from the other. A typical boundary dispute was caused by Susanna's system of rules which she had devised for the training and discipline of her children. They included a provision that no child who confessed to a wrong should be beaten for it. Samuel's quick temper was simply not equal to the strain of keeping such a rule, and Susanna years later ruefully admitted her partial failure in a letter to her son John: 'This rule prevented a great deal of lying; and would have done more, if one in the family would have observed it. But he could not be prevailed on, and therefore was often imposed upon by false colours and equivocations, which none would have used but one, had they been kindly dealt with: and some in spite of all would always speak truth plainly.'[2]

On the other hand, Samuel reacted very sharply when his wife showed the least sign of encroaching upon his clerical

[1] G. Elsie Harrison, *Son to Susanna*, p. 25.
[2] Clarke, *Wesley Family*, II, 14.

prerogatives. When Susanna took upon her to hold evening services in the rectory—Samuel being in London and his curate-in-charge notoriously negligent—her husband needed a good deal of persuasion before he decided in favour of his wife and against the curate, who had complained bitterly to Samuel of this experience of women in the ministry. Nor was it merely over practical matters of this kind that they failed to see eye to eye. They differed also on some fundamental principles of religion and politics. It was perhaps symptomatic of their deeper differences that they were unable to agree as to the best course of reading for John to follow when he was contemplating ordination. Samuel advised him to undertake a stiff course of technical theology, laying stress on the study of the biblical languages and the scholarly equipment needed by a clergyman. Susanna, whose Puritan training was far more deeply ingrained, begged to differ, and hoped that John would give his main attention to practical and experimental divinity, that is to moral and pastoral theology, in which the Puritan divines excelled.[1]

The most celebrated controversy between Samuel and Susanna, however, arose quite suddenly and unexpectedly in the year 1702. There then came to a head a sharp difference of political conviction, which was also a crisis of conscience, on which neither of them was prepared to give way. The matter in dispute touched Samuel at one of his most sensitive points, his fervent loyalty to the reigning sovereign, King William III. So strong was his attachment to the King that many years later, in his great commentary on *Job*, he introduced William, in his notes on the well-known passage describing the war-horse (*Job* 39, 19–25), as 'the fittest hero to have managed the warlike animal just described'.[2] The irrelevance of this tribute is obvious, but so too is its sincerity,

[1] See Clarke, *Wesley Family*, I, 293ff; and Tyerman, *Life and Times of the Rev. Samuel Wesley*, pp. 391–2; also *Wesley's Chapel Magazine* (Jan. 1965).
[2] Clarke, *Wesley Family*, I, 243.

for, as Adam Clarke's source adds, 'dead monarchs can give no rewards'. Both Samuel and Susanna were Tory in their politics, but whereas he accepted William III as the lawful sovereign, she held to the House of Stuart and the Divine Right of Kings. She looked upon William, the 'Prince of Orange', as she insisted on calling him, as a mere usurper. She made her attitude quite clear in one of her written meditations, in which she reflects on the Revolution of 1688, which had replaced James II by William and Mary:

Whether they did well in driving a prince from his hereditary throne, I leave to their own consciences to determine; though I cannot tell how to think that a king of England can ever be accountable to his subjects for any maladministrations or abuse of power: but as he derives his power from God, so to Him only must he answer for his using it. But still I make a great difference between those who entered into a confederacy against their prince, and those who, knowing nothing of the contrivance, and so consequently not consenting to it, only submitted to the present government,—which seems to me to be the law of the English nation, and the duty of private Christians, and the case of the generality of this people. But whether the praying for a usurper, and vindicating his usurpations after he has the throne, be not participating his sins, is easily determined.[1]

The clash between Mr and Mrs Wesley turned precisely on this point—Susanna's refusal to pray for 'a usurper', as she persisted in regarding King William. John Wesley's own account of the incident, which happened before he was born, evidently draws on the family tradition of the events:

'Sukey,' said my father to my mother one day after family prayer, 'why did you not say *amen* this morning to the prayer for the king?' 'Because,' said she, 'I do not believe the Prince of Orange to be king.' 'If that be the case,' said he, 'you and I must part; for if we have two kings, we must have two beds.' My mother was inflexible. My father went immediately to his study; and, after spending some time with himself, set out for London, where,

[1] *Wesley Banner*, (1852), IV, 283

being *convocation man* for the diocese of Lincoln, he remained without visiting his own house for the remainder of the year. On March 8th in the following year, 1702, King William died; and as both my father and mother were agreed as to the legitimacy of Queen Anne's title, the cause of their misunderstanding ceased. My father returned to Epworth, and conjugal harmony was restored.[1]

This family account which John Wesley retails, is extremely vivid and told with admirable economy, but it is inaccurate in a number of important details. Fresh manuscript evidence, in part from the pen of Susanna herself, came to light as recently as 1953, and brings the whole picture into much sharper focus. It shows that Wesley's account has on the one hand exaggerated the length of the quarrel, but on the other has seriously underestimated its gravity. The new material consists of letters which were found in an unpublished MS. book of 257 quarto pages, composed sometime in the eighteenth century, entitled 'The Genuine Remains of the Late Pious and Learned George Hickes, D.D., and Suffragan Bishop of Thetford, consisting of Controversial Letters and Other Discourses'.[2] The letters show that Susanna, in her distress at being forsaken by her husband, first turned for advice and help to her neighbour and friend, Lady Yarborough of Snaith, Yorkshire, who like herself supported the refusal of the Nonjuring clergy to take the Oath of Allegiance to William and Mary. Lady Yarborough, with Susanna's permission, laid her case of conscience before the prominent Nonjuring divine, Dr George Hickes.

The new material includes four letters written by Susanna, two to Lady Yarborough and two to Dr Hickes. They

---

[1] Clarke, *Wesley Family*, I, 198–9. This account, given by John Wesley to Adam Clarke, is the fuller of two which he records. For the other, see *Arminian Magazine* (1786), p. 606, and Wesley, *Works*, XIII, 504.

[2] The material was first published in the *Manchester Guardian*, on 2nd and 3rd July, 1953, and then reprinted in *Proceedings of the Wesley Historical Society*, Vol. XXIX, Pt. 3 (Sept. 1953), pp. 50ff.

movingly reflect her acute distress of mind. Torn between her loyalty to conscience and her feelings as wife and mother, she was by no means so 'inflexible' as John's account suggests. She wrote to Lady Yarborough on March 7th, 1702, soon after the trouble began:

I'm almost ashamed to own what extreme disturbance this accident has given me, yet I value not the world. I value neither reputation, friends, or anything in comparison of the single satisfaction, of preserving a conscience void of offence towards God and man; and how I can do that if I mock almighty God, by begging pardon for what I think no sin, is past my discerning. But I am inexpressibly miserable, for I can see no possibility of reconciling these differences, though I would submit to anything in the world to oblige him to live in the house with me. I appeal to your Ladyship if my circumstances are not strangely unhappy. I believe myself an Original of misery.[1]

The day after Susanna wrote this letter, King William III died, but his death did *not*—contrary to John's account— alter the rector's attitude. He had sworn with an oath, and would not be moved. Susanna graphically recounts his rash oath in her letter to Lady Yarborough:

'Tis but a little while since he one evening observed in our Family prayers I did not say Amen to his prayer for K W [King William] as I usually do to all others; upon which he retired to his study, and calling me to him asked me the reason of my not saying Amen to the Prayer. I was a little surprised at the question and don't well know what I answered, but too too well I remember what followed: He immediately kneeled down and imprecated the divine Vengeance upon himself and all his posterity if ever he touched me more or came into a bed with me before I had begged God's pardon and his, for not saying Amen to the prayer for the Kg.[2]

In a second letter to Lady Yarborough, written on March 15th, 1702, Susanna makes clear that the King's death has left the situation unchanged: 'I've represented as long as I could be heard the sin of the Oath and ill consequences of

[1] *Proceedings of the Wesley Historical Society*, XXIX, Pt. 3, p. 52.
[2] Ibid., loc. cit.

it to my Master, but he cannot be convinced he has done ill, nor does the present change in State (the King's death on March 8) make any alteration in his mind; I am persuaded nothing but an omnipotent power can move him and there I leave it. He is for London at Easter where he designs to try if he can get a Chaplain's place in a Man of War.'[1]

How seriously Samuel intended this threat to go back to sea, where he had begun his ministry, it is difficult to say; but Susanna faced up to it as a real possibility, with a resigned faith which shows how deep the difference between them had gone: 'I'm more easy in the thoughts of parting because I think we are not likely to live happily together. I have six very little children, which though he tells me he will take good care of, yet if anything should befall him at Sea we should be in no very good condition, but still I believe that that charitable Being which feeds the Ravens and cloathes the Lilies will never think me or mine below his care and Providence, though none in the world is more unworthy of either.' She went on to add that she had told Samuel she would accept the judgement of two referees in the matter, provided she were allowed to choose one of them, but he would not. At Easter, April 5th, Samuel left for London, and shortly after Susanna consulted the Nonjuring Bishop, Dr George Hickes, with whom she had been put in touch by Lady Yarborough.

The advice of Dr Hickes, who had been deprived of his preferments for his conscientious refusal to take the Oath of Allegiance to William and Mary in 1690, can well be imagined. Yet before examining it in detail, it is well to realize the outstanding calibre of the ecclesiastic whom Susanna had consulted in her moral dilemma. Professor David Douglas, in a most engaging sketch of his life and learning, calls Hickes, 'probably the most remarkable figure

[1] *Proceedings of W.H.S.*, XXIX, Pt. 3, p. 53.

among the English historical scholars of his time', who exercised over his fellow-historians an hegemony based not only on profound scholarship, but also on 'the courage which he displayed in adversity . . . as a proscribed rebel and as a hunted fugitive'.[1] After being dispossessed as Dean of Worcester, Hickes nailed to the gates of his cathedral a defiant protest, in which he claimed, 'I was, and still do continue, the only Rightful and Legal Dean of this Cathedral Church of Worcester; and that I do not any way relinquish my said Title, but shall, God willing, use all just Means which the Laws of this Realm allow for the Preservation and Recovery thereof. . .'[2] This act made Hickes a hunted outlaw in constant danger of death. He was a man of immense courage and tenacity in holding to conviction, and Susanna could have found no one better qualified to steel her in her loyalty to her own conscience than George Hickes.

In April 1702, Susanna wrote to Hickes, addressing him as 'the Revd Mr Dean Hickes', and laying her quandary before him. She told him that her husband,

is now for referring the whole to the Archbishop of York and Bishop of Lincoln, and says if I will not be determined by them, he will do anything rather than live with a person that is the declared enemy of his country, which he believes himself obliged to love before all the world.

I very well know before such Judges I'm sure to be condemned without a fair hearing; nor can I see any reason I have to ask either God Almighty's or his pardon for acting according to the best knowledge I have of things of that nature. If I thought or could be persuaded I'm in an error I would freely retract it and ask his pardon before the whole world. He accuses me of pride and obstinacy and insists upon my making him satisfaction for the injury he believes I've done him. I dare not plead not guilty to such an Indictment, but yet I hope however I may in other instances be culpable, in this I'm pretty innocent . . .[3]

There is surely a revelation in this letter of the characters of

---

[1] David C. Douglas, *English Scholars 1660–1730* (revised edn. 1951), p. 77.
[2] Douglas, op. cit., p. 81.
[3] *Proceedings of W.H.S.*, XXIX, Pt. 3, p. 54.

the parties to the dispute. Samuel, with conscious rectitude, 'accuses' Susanna of 'pride and obstinacy'. She in turn does not, as he certainly would have done had the positions been reversed, round on him with a *tu quoque*, and point to the beam in his own eye. Instead, with disarming humility, she simply acknowledges, 'I dare not plead not guilty to such an Indictment', and will claim no more than that, on the main count, she is 'pretty innocent'. Had she been a person of a different nature, she might well have stood amazed at her own moderation.

Dr Hickes replied on 29th April, giving his judgement decidedly in Susanna's favour. Samuel's oath he held to be inconsistent with his marriage vows, and therefore quite invalid,—'it was perjury in him to make it, and will be a continuance of perjury for him to persist in the performance of it.' He advised Susanna to consult the Archbishop of York and the Bishop of Lincoln, and request them, if they agreed that the oath was unlawful, to 'charge him to loose himself from the bond of sin, by which he cannot bind himself by the law of God and Man . . .' He encouraged her, even if this fresh move should fail, to stand firm, at whatever cost, concluding his advice, 'Wherefore good Madam, stick to God and your conscience which are your best friends, whatever you may suffer for adhering to them.' Hickes's own life gave him the moral authority to proffer such counsel, grave as the result of following it might be; and such an appeal would hardly be lost on the daughter of Samuel Annesley, another sufferer for conscience's sake. She replied at the end of July, disclosing how near to submission she had been when Hickes's letter came, and revealing several unexpected turns in the domestic situation:

My Master was then at London and had given me time to consider what to do, whether I would submit to his judgement and implicitly obey him in matters of conscience. I foresaw a great many evils would inevitably befal me if I refused to satisfy his desires, and had scarce courage enough to support me in the melancholy prospect when your Letter came, which was the noblest cordial, and gave me the greatest satisfaction of anything in my whole life. When he returned he absolutely refused a reference, and so I thought it unnecessary to write to the Archbishop. He stayed two days and then left me early one morning with a resolution never to see me more, but the infinite Power that disposes and overrules the minds of men as he pleases, and can speak to their wild unreasonable passions as he does to the waves of the sea, hitherto shalt thou go and no farther, so ordered it, that in his way he met a Clergyman to whom he communicated his intentions, and the reason that induced him to leave his Family: He extremely pitied him and condemned me, but however, he prevailed with him to return.[1]

Perhaps Samuel, for all his bluster about never seeing his wife again, did not need much persuading to return, but the unknown clergyman's tactful words helped to begin the healing of the breach. Susanna's letter ended with a reference to 'a new misfortune' in the shape of a fire which had destroyed two-thirds of the parsonage house. In view of Samuel's rash oath, she was driven to see in this disaster heaven's rebuke to him, and to say, 'This is the finger of God.' Whether or not this was the fire of the Lord, its fall upon his household shook Samuel, and melted the hard stubborn pride which had kept him from his wife. They began life together again in the ruined rectory, and within the following year, on the 17th June 1703, the child of their reconciliation was born: John Benjamin Wesley. It would have been a barren quarrel indeed which had deprived the world of that new life.

This quarrel and its mending have deserved detailed treatment, because of their paramount interest for an understanding of the marital relationship of Samuel and Susanna. It would be misleading, however, to suggest or imply that their married life was at best a state of armed neutrality or of continual, if subdued, conflict. Samuel's picture of their early married life was no doubt idealized, but both at the time of

[1] *Proceedings of W.H.S.*, XXIX, Pt. 3, p. 55.

writing and throughout their union it bore some real relation to the truth. To continue the quotation from his poem where previously it was broken off,[1] we may grant the sincerity of Samuel's claim:

> Nor did I for her care ungrateful prove,
> But only used my power to shew my love:
> Whate'er she asked I gave, without reproach or grudge,
> For still she reason asked,—and I was judge:
> All my commands requests at her fair hands,
> And her requests to me, were all commands:
> To others' thresholds rarely she'd incline;
> Her house her pleasure was, and she was mine;
> Rarely abroad, or never but with me,
> Or when by pity called, or charity.[2]

However much his own practical inefficiency added to the burden of his wife's housekeeping, it could not truly be said that Samuel was unaware of her worth. He was sufficiently apprised of the realities of daily living to know that he had married a wife of remarkable courage and competence. While imprisoned in Lincoln Castle, he confessed in a letter to the Archbishop of York, 'One of my biggest concerns was my being forced to leave my poor lambs in the midst of so many wolves. But the great Shepherd is able to provide for them, and to preserve them. My wife bears it with that courage which becomes her, and which I expected from her.'[3]

For her part, Susanna was fully sensible of her husband's genuine gifts of piety and devotion. Writing to her schoolboy son, Samuel, in about 1706, she held up his father as a model, in a letter which breathes her characteristic humility, reminding him, 'You had the example of a father that had served God from his youth; and though I cannot commend my own to you, for it is too bad to be imitated, yet surely

---

[1] See above, p. 84.

[2] Samuel Wesley, *The Life of our Blessed Lord and Saviour Jesus Christ* (1693), p. 40.

[3] Clarke, *Wesley Family*, II, 213.

earnest prayers many years, and some little good advice has
not been wanting.'[1] As will appear, what she modestly calls,
'some little good advice', covered a most thorough training
in manners, morals, and religion; and she certainly underestimated the importance of her own example for her
children. Yet at least her words make quite plain the high
regard she had for her husband. We have seen how quickly
she sprang to his defence when her brother cast aspersions on
his business integrity.[2] For all his faults, she remained
intensely loyal to him, and was quite distraught when he was
overtaken by his last illness. Charles wrote to his elder
brother Samuel in March 1735, 'My father declines so fast
that before next year he will in all probability be at his
journey's end; so that I must see him now, or never more
with my bodily eyes. My mother seems more cast down at
the apprehension of his death than I thought she could have
been; and what is still worse, he seems so too.'[3] He died in
fact the following month, in the full assurance of faith, and
in his epitaph Susanna emphasized the one element in their
life on which, for all their differences, they had never been
divided. She chose to underline as the central fact of her
husband's life that Trinitarian faith to which he had brought
her, which had become a bond between them at the time of
their first love, and which still united them: 'As he lived so he
died in the true Catholic Faith of the Holy Trinity in unity,
and that Jesus Christ is God Incarnate; and the only Saviour
of Mankind.'

[1] *The Arminian Magazine*, XI (1788), p. 85.
[2] See above, p. 70.
[3] Frank Baker, *Charles Wesley as revealed in his letters*, p. 19.

CHAPTER FOUR

A Mother In Israel

The chief part of family care and government con-
sisteth in the right education of children. *Richard
Baxter*

THE Book of Proverbs characterizes the virtuous
woman as one who, 'openeth her mouth with wisdom; and in
her tongue is the law of kindness. She looketh well to the ways
of her household, and eateth not the bread of idleness. Her
children arise up, and call her blessed; her husband also,
and he praiseth her.'[1] Susanna Wesley probably came as
near to embodying this scriptural ideal of the good wife and
mother as mortal woman ever has done; and her father's old
friend Richard Baxter would certainly have rejoiced at the
great pains she took over 'family care and government'. In
this prime matter, she makes clear that her whole 'method'—
the word is her own—was devoted to the one supreme end
of saving her children's souls. Her concentration and single-
ness of purpose were quite extraordinary, as indeed they
needed to be, for she had to face numerous handicaps and

[1] Proverbs 31 : 26ff.

disabilities. If she had had nothing to do except manage her household and educate her children, she would have had more than enough. She bore nineteen children, and ten of them, three boys and seven girls, survived infancy. They were lively children and quite sufficient to keep her fully occupied, but while her husband was in London for Convocation,[1] she had to do her best to supply his place as well. She had to keep an eye on the parish, oversee the cultivation of the glebe-land belonging to the rectory, manage the family finances, and keep her husband informed by letter of the state of affairs at home.

Nor was it simply a physical burden of work which Susanna carried. She had also to contend with the cares of poverty and debt. Whether or not, as Samuel's poem declared, 'In our low house, there was no room for pride,' there was certainly none for extravagance. Every penny counted, and waste was a luxury which could not be tolerated. It may well be that John Wesley's lasting concern for the poor owes a good deal to his being the child of a poor home himself. He grew up in a house where the pressure of debt was one of the constants of daily life, and a sore trial to his mother. In 1705, with her husband in jail for debt, she was reduced to extremities. She describes an interview she had with John Sharp, the Archbishop of York: ' "Tell me," said he, "Mrs Wesley, whether you ever really wanted bread?" "My lord," said I, "I will freely own to your grace that, strictly speaking, I never did want bread. But then, I had so much care to get it before it was eat, and to pay for it after, as has often made it very unpleasant to me. And I think to have bread on such terms is the next degree of wretchedness to having none at all!" '[2] Archbishop Sharp agreed, and gave her a generous money gift to tide her over this crisis.

[1] As he was for several months during the years 1701 and 1702.
[2] Clarke, *Wesley Family*, I, 391.

Susanna's cares and troubles pressed so heavily upon her, that at times they crept into her prayers and devotions. She became so preoccupied with making ends meet, so careful for food and clothing, that at one point she became convinced that she had fallen prey to covetousness. She probed herself with the scalpel of self-examination, and asked: 'Since you seem to me to have desired no more than a competency of the things of this world, no more but only what was sufficient to preserve you from want and debt . . . how were you guilty of covetousness in those desires?' Her scrupulous conscience, unwilling to acquit her, pointed out that, 'we may be in some degree guilty of that sin, when our desires of necessaries, or conveniencies are attended with anxiety and uneasiness of mind.' Her evening meditation crystallized her conviction that, by having her 'thoughts . . . too much upon the things of this world', she had been guilty 'of some degree of covetousness and idolatry'. The next day, she administered the self-reproof: 'You must in the first place examine your self whether you love riches or honour &c., so much as to be the least uneasy without them.'[1]

The temptation of a poor parson's wife to pay undue regard to riches and honour may seem at first sight quite unreal. Yet Susanna was not only a poor parson's wife. She was the daughter of a distinguished and quite wealthy London divine. As Dr Annesley's daughter, she had enjoyed a modest share of the riches and honour that were his. She found very little of either at Epworth, and it was natural that the contrast with her former station in life should tempt her to feel dissatisfied and resentful. The strain her circumstances imposed on her shows through another meditation, where she records her disappointment at being plunged into money troubles again, just as she seemed about to get clear of them for a time:

[1] Headingley MSS, A. ff. 138ff.

99

Evening. You had long hoped and expected by your care, frugality, and industry to have provided amply for the ensuing summer, and thought that such a sum which you believed you should receive upon account would infallibly prevent the pressures you lay under last year. Upon review of income and exits you find yourself greatly disappointed and that all your prospects of ease and plenty was but a dream, and after all you are like to be involved in greater difficulties than your boasted prudence could foresee. This hath somewhat discomposed your mind and hath disposed it to that anxiety about the things of this world that in obedience to the command of Jesus Christ you have resolvedly avoided for some time . . .

She did not, however, give way to recrimination, but instead thanked God for this 'dispensation of his providence', which had given her, 'a sight and sense of some sins which before I could not have imagined I was in the least inclined to, namely of idolatry and covetousness, and want of practical submission to the will of God'.[1]

Inevitably at times she longed to be free of the continual care and bustle of the household, as when she confided to her devotional journal: 'Were I permitted to choose a state of life, or, positively to ask of God any thing in this world, I would humbly choose, and beg that I might be placed in such a station wherein I might have daily bread with moderate care, without so much hurry, and distraction; and that I might have more leisure to retire from the world, without injuring my —— (?husband)[2] or children. Nor should any consideration of interest, of riches, honour, pleasure, prevail upon me, to encumber myself with such a multiplicity of business, as I now submit to, only in obedience to the order of Divine Providence.' Yet even at this point, she had the insight and the grace to add, 'I do not know whether such a state of life would really be best for me: nor am I assured that if I had more leisure, I should be more zealously devoted to God, and serve him better than

[1] Headingley MSS, A. ff. 136–7. For Susanna's three daily periods of meditation, morning, noon, and evening, see below, p. 136.

[2] Susanna often leaves a blank instead of a proper name or personal reference.

now.'[1] The same pressure of material cares led her in 1727, when she had spent more than thirty years in her struggle at Epworth, to make a vow after the manner of the Patriarch Jacob. She promised, 'If it will please God indeed to bless me, and . . . if he will vouchsafe to give me food to eat, and raiment to put on, without debt, without this extreme distress, then will I offer up myself absolutely, entirely to Jesus Christ, the Incarnate God, only Saviour of the world!'[2]

Yet her struggle against poverty was only part of the story. It might be thought, from the sheer amount of work which Susanna managed to accomplish, that she was the tireless kind, a robust, hearty, indefatigable woman. She was nothing of the sort. In addition to the strain of incessant childbearing, she had constantly to contend with physical weakness. Her wrestling with domestic and financial difficulties was accompanied by a life-long battle against ill-health. In the words of her husband, for a considerable part of her life, she was ailing for half the year. Her reaction to bodily pain was to make a renewed effort to submit her will to God, and so strive to make physical trials yield some spiritual fruit. In one of her meditations, she recorded: 'Often interrupted by bodily infirmities indeed. Yet such is the will of God; therefore, in this case, your duty is patience and submission. Still remember, obedience is better than sacrifice.'[3] Because of her poor health, she made it a rule, 'never to drink anything strong, but merely for refreshment.' So we find her in one morning meditation reprimanding herself for 'drinking twice of ale in so short a time', and going on to make her delicate constitution a ground for thanksgiving: 'You have great reason to adore the great and good God, that hath given you so nice a constitution, as will not bear the least degree of intemperance. He might have made

[1] Headingley MSS, A. f. 17f.
[2] Headingley MSS, A. end papers (unfoliated).
[3] Headingley MSS, A. f. 40.

you strong to endure the excesses others run into, and so you might often have been exposed to temptations to offend, whereas now you are doubly guarded, both by his wise and holy laws, and an infirm body. Glory be to Thee, O Lord!'[1] The absence of self-pity, and the determination to extract positive good from her infirmity, are both typical of Susanna. After a disturbed night's rest, she deals very sternly with herself for being so upset by it: 'If a little pain, or an uneasy bed, be so tiresome for one night, what will you do if God in his infinite wisdom should think fit to afflict you with a long or very painful sickness before he takes you out of the world?'[2]

Susanna rarely refers to her ailments in her letter, but twice in 1732, while writing to her son John, she does so. In February, she speaks of knowing from experience the state in which, 'every member of the body is the seat of pain;'[3] while in October she explains briefly that she would have written sooner, but for 'pain of body and other severer trials not convenient to mention'.[4] On another occasion she describes herself as 'one that, by sickness, is compelled to spend great part of her time in a chamber'.[5] According to one of her daughters, this ill-health was 'often occasioned by want of clothes or convenient meat', but Susanna herself refrains from any such complaint. John seriously thought that illness would carry her off in middle life; but her frailty was more than compensated by the indomitable will which helped to carry her to the end of a long and ceaselessly active life.

It was not only a busy life, but an anxious one, its surface often ruffled by the winds of circumstance. Debts and duties, sickness and cares, crowded in upon her, and sometimes, as

[1] Headingley MSS, A. f. 45.
[2] Ibid., A. f. 57.
[3] Stevenson, *Memorials of the Wesley Family*, p. 167.
[4] Clarke, *Wesley Family*, II, 100.
[5] Ibid., I, 388.

we have seen, thrust themselves into the sanctuary of her
inner life. Yet for the most part her interior life of disciplined devotion provided her with a depth of peace and calm
which worldly care could not finally undermine. John Wesley
was later to describe, as he looked back to his childhood,
'the calm serenity with which his mother transacted business,
wrote letters, and conversed, surrounded by her thirteen
children.'[1] When the crisis of 1705, leading to her husband's
imprisonment for debt, broke upon the family, one of the
most impressive features of the whole episode was the serene
courage of Susanna. Just before Samuel was arrested in the
June, she had the mortification of losing her three-weeks' old
baby, through a violent popular outburst against her husband for supporting the Tory candidates in the county
elections. Samuel described the events in a letter to Archbishop Sharp, dated 7th June 1705:

I went to Lincoln on Tuesday night, May 29th; and the election
began on Wednesday, 30th. A great part of the night our Isle
people kept drumming, shouting, and firing of pistols and guns
under the window where my wife lay; who had been brought to
bed not three weeks. I had put the child to nurse over against my
own house: the noise kept his nurse waking till one or two in the
morning. Then they left off; and the nurse being heavy with
sleep, overlaid the child. She waked; and finding it dead, ran
over with it to my house, almost distracted; and calling my
servants, threw it into their arms. They, as wise as she, ran up
with it to my wife; and before she was well awake threw it cold
and dead into hers. She composed herself as well as she could, and
that day got it buried.[2]

The experience was horrible enough in all conscience, and
to make it worse her husband was away in Lincoln, and the
Epworth mob still kept up their callous racket, even after
the child had died. Samuel went on to describe the brutal
threats of the 'Isle men' against him and his children. It was
rumoured that a gang of them had vowed, 'If they got me

[1] Clarke, *Wesley Family*, II, 7.
[2] Clarke, *Wesley Family*, I, 211.

in the castle yard, they would squeeze my guts out'; while, when he got home, 'they sent the drum and mob, with guns, &c., as usual, to compliment me till after midnight. One of them passing by on Friday evening, and seeing my children in the yard, cried out, "O ye devils! we will come and turn ye all out of doors a begging shortly." ' These trials, with the impending imprisonment of her husband hanging over her head, might well have reduced a lesser woman to a state of nervous collapse. Yet Samuel, though himself 'disturbed and disordered' in mind, could report to the Archbishop, 'All this, thank God, does not in the least sink my wife's spirits.'[1]

Three months later Samuel wrote to the Archbishop from Lincoln Castle, on the 12th of September, describing another cowardly attack on his 'forlorn family' by the Isle men: 'The other matter is concerning the stabbing my cows in the night since I came hither, but a few weeks ago; and endeavouring thereby to starve my forlorn family in my absence; my cows being all dried by it, which was their chief subsistence; though I hope they had not the power to kill any of them outright.' Yet still Susanna managed to bear up: ' 'Tis not every one could bear these things,' wrote Samuel with a world of under-statement, 'but, I bless God, my wife is less concerned with suffering them than I am in the writing, or than I believe your Grace will be in reading them.'[2] Five days later he wrote to thank the Archbishop for his financial help, and disclosed how, on his first coming to the jail, his wife had sent him all the realizable wealth she had: 'My Lord, I am so full of God's mercies that neither my eyes nor heart can hold them. When I came hither, my stock was but little above ten shillings, and my wife's at home scarce so much. She soon sent me her rings, because she had nothing else to relieve me with; but I returned them, and God soon

[1] Clarke, *Wesley Family*, I, 211–12.
[2] Clarke, *Wesley Family*, I, 217.

provided for me.'[1] His spirit in many ways matched hers, and he too could rise magnanimously to the occasion; but there is no doubt that in this crisis of the family fortunes, it was Susanna who bore the brunt. She had to keep the home going and make ends meet. She had to face the attacks of the Epworth louts upon their property. Samuel, lodged in his debtors' prison, but still able to continue his pastoral ministry there, was at least free of all that. Her rings may have been all she had to relieve him with, in a tangible sense; but it must have been an untold relief to Samuel to know that, as he testified himself, 'My wife bears it with that courage which becomes her, and which I expected from her.'[2]

Despite poverty, sickness, and extraneous misfortune, Susanna managed her large household with conspicuous success. She did more. She devised a careful system of religious training for her children, whose spiritual nurture she looked upon as a sacred trust. Richard Baxter, one of her favourite authors, admirably expresses the profound sense of responsibility for her children's spiritual welfare which inspired her efforts. In a section of *The Saints' Everlasting Rest*, Baxter urges parents to face up to their spiritual duties, and points out that mothers are in a specially advantageous position in this matter: 'Especially you, mothers, remember this; you are more with your children while they are little ones than their fathers, be you therefore still teaching them as soon as ever they are capable of learning. You cannot do God such eminent service yourselves as men, but you may train up children that may do it, and then you will have part of the comfort and honour . . . What a deal of pains you are at with the bodies of your children more than the fathers, and what do you suffer to bring them into the world; and will you not be at as much pains for the saving their souls? You are naturally of more tender affections than men; and

[1] Ibid., I, 220.
[2] Ibid., I, 213.

will it not move you to think that your children should perish for ever? Oh, therefore, I beseech you, for the sake of the children of your bowels, teach them, admonish them, watch over them, and give them no rest till you have brought them over to Christ.'[1]

It is quite likely that Susanna had read these words of Baxter;[2] but whether she had or not, they express precisely the spirit in which she embarked on the Christian nurture of her family. In 1709 she wrote to her son Samuel, 'There is nothing I now desire to live for but to do some small service to my children; that as I have brought them into the world, I may, if it please God, be an instrument of doing good to their souls.'[3] She mentioned that she had for some years been compiling a 'little manual' of instruction in the Christian faith, for her children's use; but that all her writings had been destroyed when their house was burned down in that same year. In 1712, however, she wrote another treatise for the use of her children, and prefaced it with a text which echoes Baxter's concern: 'I write unto you little children, of whom I travail in birth again, until Christ be formed in you.'[4] In this spirit she devised a careful system of religious training for her children, who were put into, 'a regular method of living' from babyhood. As soon as they reached their fifth birthday, Susanna put them to school in the house, and herself taught them their letters and their faith for six hours a day. How did she manage it, with all her other commitments? The key to her success was her 'method'. She worked to rule,—though in anything but a trade-union sense. The only way in which she was able to give so thorough a training to her large brood of children, was by carefully dividing her day according to an ordered timetable, and by

---

[1] Baxter, *Practical Works*, (ed. Orme), XXIII, 154–5.
[2] See below, p. 138.
[3] Clarke, *Wesley Family*, II, 32f.
[4] *W.H.S. Pubns.*, No. 3, Mrs Wesley's Conference with her Daughter (1898), p. 5.

placing the children's education high on her list of priorities. In his sermon to the House of Commons many years before, her father had asked the Members pointedly, 'What are you in matters of religion, and the power of godliness?' and again, 'What are you in your Families? Are they well-ordered (little) Common-wealths, well-disciplined Churches?' Susanna's household was a choice example of both.

When another Puritan divine, Timothy Rogers, preached at the funeral of Susanna's sister, Elizabeth, in 1697, he gave some advice which Susanna could not have followed more closely had he given it to her personally. He stressed that, 'Mothers may do great Service to Religion, by leaving good Advices to their Children,' and developed his point in a way that was prophetic of Susanna's efforts: 'If good Women would apply themselves to reading and study, as the Men do, or had equal Advantage for Knowledge in their Education, no doubt we should have more of their excellent Composures, many of them have an happy Genius, and a smooth Expression, and might write as well as work, and the Pen might have as good success as the Needle; especially, they may make Observations, or draw up Rules for the good order of their own Families, and when they see fit, communicate them for the Good of others.'[1]

Mrs Wesley, wittingly or not, took this typically Puritan piece of advice, and drew up a set of rules for her family. She also saw fit to 'communicate them for the Good of others', when in 1732 her son John asked her for a precise account of her educational practice, for his own guidance. The opening paragraph of her detailed reply, written on 24th July 1732, is typical:

Dear Son,
According to your desire, I have collected the principal rules I observed in educating my family.
The children were always put into a regular method of living,

[1] T. Rogers, *The Character of a Good Woman*, pp. 48f.

in such things as they were capable of, from their birth; as in dressing and undressing, changing their linen, &c. The first quarter commonly passes in sleep. After that, they were, if possible, laid into their cradle awake, and rocked to sleep; and so they were kept rocking till it was time for them to awake. This was done to bring them to a regular course of sleeping, which at first was three hours in the morning, and three in the afternoon; afterwards two hours, till they needed none at all. When turned a year old (and some before), they were taught to fear the rod, and to cry softly, by which means they escaped abundance of correction which they might otherwise have had; and that most odious noise of the crying of children was rarely heard in the house, but the family usually lived in as much quietness as if there had not been a child among them.[1]

Susanna's competence is vouched for by one of her grand-children, Samuel, the son of Charles Wesley, who in some manuscript memoirs writes of her:

My Grandmother . . . was a Person of great literary Attainment, and herself educated her numerous family until they were grown up. She had the happy Talent of imbuing their Minds with every Species of useful Knowledge, and in a Method which left all that was taught indelibly imprest on their Memory.
She had a Room appropriate for this Purpose, and accustomed each Child to communicate to another whatever he or she had gained from its Mother; and what was most remarkable they never suffered Punishment from the Rod; for from their Infancy they had been taught to fear it, and cry softly, so that a Finger held up was sufficient to restrain or correct whatever was deserving Animadversion.[2]

The substance of this paragraph is found in Susanna's own account, but the two details of the separate schoolroom and Susanna's warning finger most probably represent the reminiscence of Charles rather than the embellishment of his son.

Order and restraint were the hallmarks of the Wesley household, as Susanna's description of the children's be-haviour at meals makes plain. They learned to eat whatever was set before them at 'their little table', which was 'set by

[1] Clarke, *Wesley Family*, II, 9.
[2] British Museum Additional MSS 27, 593. f. 1.

ours, where they could be overlooked'; and were taught never to shout for what they wanted, but make whispered requests through the maid. The maid put them all to bed between seven and eight o'clock, and left them to go to sleep on their own, 'for there was no such thing allowed of, in our house, as sitting by a child till it fell asleep.'[1] They were trained to be courteous, both to the servants and to one another: 'They were quickly made to understand they might have nothing they cried for, and instructed to speak handsomely for what they wanted. They were not suffered to ask even the lowest servant for aught, without saying, Pray give me such a thing; and the servant was chid if she ever let them omit that word.' They were not allowed 'to call each other by their proper names without the addition of brother or sister'. (John Wesley's use of 'Brother' and 'Sister' for the members of the Methodist Societies, went back not only to the New Testament Church, but to the family life of Epworth rectory.)

The fact that the children were taught at home did not mean that they escaped the disciplines of school. On the contrary, for six hours a day they applied themselves steadily to their lessons, and their studies rapidly bore fruit. Susanna describes the regime:

There was no such thing as loud talking or playing allowed of; but every one was kept close to business for the six hours of school. And it is almost incredible what a child may be taught in a quarter of a year by a vigorous application, if it have but a tolerable capacity and good health. Kezzy excepted, all could read better in that time, than the most of women can do as long as they live. Rising out of their places, or going out of the room, was not permitted, except for good cause; and running into the yard, garden, or street, without leave, was always esteemed a capital offence.[2]

In ethos the rectory resembled a small private boarding

---

[1] Clarke, *Wesley Family*, II, 10.
[2] Clarke, *Wesley Family*, II, 13.

school, for Susanna took good care, as this extract shows, to isolate her children from the rough crude life of the parish. All went well until the fire of 1709, which not only burned down the rectory, but scattered the children and threatened to undo much of Susanna's training. Sukey and Hetty went to live for a time with their Uncle Matthew Wesley, a London doctor, but the others were boarded out with folk in the village, from whom they learned an unaccustomed freedom and a very different code of behaviour from the one their mother had instilled into them. Susanna's chagrin can be imagined, and even shows through her objective account of the sequence of events:

For some years we went on very well. Never were children in better order. Never were children better disposed to piety, or in more subjection to their parents, till that fatal dispersion of them after the fire, into several families. In those they were left at full liberty to converse with servants, which before they had always been restrained from; and to run abroad to play with any children, good or bad. They soon learned to neglect a strict observance of the Sabbath; and got knowledge of several songs and bad things, which before they had no notion of. That civil behaviour, which made them admired when they were at home, by all who saw them, was in a great measure lost; and a clownish accent and many rude ways were learnt, which were not reformed without some difficulty.

Her observation that their habits 'were not reformed without some difficulty', is no doubt a characteristic understatement. Compared to what they had been, Susanna's children were evidently beginning to run wild. The Lincolnshire accent which they had picked up was only a token of a general deterioration of their manners which had set in; but to Susanna the situation was merely a challenge, to be taken up at once. She soon had them back to their former ways, and even added improvements to her system. She began to enlist the aid of the older children in helping to train the younger ones, and described the 'strict reform' she entered on when the family were together again in their new house:

'Then was begun the custom of singing psalms at beginning and leaving school morning and evening. Then also that of a general retirement at five o'clock was entered upon. When the oldest took the youngest that could speak, and the second the next, to whom they read the psalms for the day, and a chapter in the New Testament: as in the morning they were directed to read the psalms, and a chapter in the Old; after which they went to their private prayers, before they got their breakfast, or came into the family.'[1]

The memory of this fire and the burning of their old home, must have stamped itself indelibly on the minds of the Wesley children. We may trace the fire's after-effects in John's description of himself as 'a brand plucked from the burning', and in the flame of the Spirit which is such a constant motif in Charles's hymns. For Susanna too the fire was a turning point. The family reform she instituted once they were settled in the new house, was carried forward by theological treatises, which she wrote for her children's benefit, and by regular weekly interviews in which she gave each child personal instruction in the Faith. She resolved to take special care of John, who had been so providentially rescued from the blaze just before the roof fell in. On 17th May 1711, as part of her evening meditation, and under the heading of 'S.J.' (Son John), she vowed to God, 'I would, if I durst, humbly offer Thee myself and all that Thou hast given me, and I would resolve (Oh give me grace to do it) that the residue of my life shall be all devoted to thy service; and I do intend to be more particularly careful of the soul of this child that Thou hast so mercifully provided for, than ever I have been, that I may do my endeavour to instil into his mind the principles of thy true religion and virtue. Lord, give me grace to do it sincerely, and prudently, and bless my attempts with good success.'[2]

[1] Clarke, *Wesley Family*, II, 13f.
[2] Headingley MSS, A. f. 65f.

In her family, Susanna had eight rules or 'bye-laws', which constituted a kind of children's charter at Epworth, and which show an unusual degree of enlightened common sense and understanding of the child mind. She detailed them for John's benefit, though it is hard to believe that he had quite forgotten these eight pillars of wisdom from the world of his childhood:

There were several bye-laws observed among us. I mention them here because I think them useful.

1. It had been observed that cowardice and fear of punishment often lead children into lying; till they get a custom of it which they cannot leave. To prevent this, a law was made that whoever was charged with a fault, of which they were guilty, if they would ingenuously confess it, and promise to amend, should not be beaten . . .

2. That no sinful action, as lying, pilfering at Church or on the Lord's-day, disobedience, quarrelling, &c., should ever pass unpunished.

3. That no child should ever be chid or beat twice for the same fault; and that, if they amended, they should never be upbraided with it afterwards.

4. That every signal act of obedience, especially when it crossed upon their own inclinations, should be always commended, and frequently rewarded, according to the merits of the case.

5. That if ever any child performed an act of obedience, or did any thing with an intention to please, though the performance was not well, yet the obedience and intention should be kindly accepted, and the child with sweetness directed how to do better for the future.

6. That propriety[1] be inviolably preserved; and none suffered to invade the property of another in the smallest matter, though it were but of the value of a farthing, or a pin; which they might not take from the owner without, much less against, his consent. This rule can never be too much inculcated on the minds of children; and from the want of parents or governors doing it as they ought, proceeds that shameful neglect of justice which we may observe in the world.

7. That promises be strictly observed; and a gift once bestowed, and so the right passed away from the donor, be not resumed, but left to the disposal of him to whom it was given;

[1] I.e. property rights.

unless it were conditional, and the condition of the obligation not performed.

8. That no girl be taught to work till she can read very well; and then that she be kept to her work with the same application, and for the same time, that she was held to in reading. This rule also is much to be observed; for the putting children to learn sewing before they can read perfectly is the very reason why so few women can read fit to be heard, and never to be well understood.[1]

Yet if these 'bye-laws' seem liberal and enlightened, Mrs Wesley's description of the essential preliminary to her system of training, has led some to stigmatize her whole 'method' as cruel and reactionary. This judgement rests upon one section of the letter, which to the unsympathetic reader may well suggest that Susanna's children had imposed upon them a joyless and repressive regime, with the fear of 'the rod' dominating their lives from babyhood onwards. The passage merits quotation in full:

In order to form the minds of children, the first thing to be done is to conquer their will, and bring them to an obedient temper. To inform the understanding is a work of time; and must with children proceed by slow degrees, as they are able to bear it: but the subjecting the will is a thing which must be done at once, and the sooner the better; for by neglecting timely correction, they will contract a stubbornness and obstinacy which are hardly ever after conquered, and never without using such severity as would be as painful to me as to the child.

Her aversion from severity, which is apparent here as it is in the 'bye-laws', is confirmed by a passage in one of her meditations. In one of her daily pauses for devotions at noon, and possibly after having dealt rather sharply with one of the children, she warns herself: 'Never correct your children to satisfy your passions, but out of a sense of your duty to reclaim them from their errors, and to preserve your authority. And then be exceeding careful to let the measure of correction, be proportionable to the fault. Make great

[1] Clarke, *Wesley Family*, II, 14f. Note the typically eighteenth century emphasis, of the 'bye-laws' on obedience, truthfulness, good faith and rights of property.

allowances for the weakness of their reason, and immaturity of their judgements.'[1] Her qualifying clause—'but never spare them through foolish fondness when they sin against God'—does not contradict the mild tenor of the passage, but confirms that she found such 'foolish fondness' as great a temptation as most parents who love their children.

Susanna contrasts her own consistent firmness with the indulgence which passes for kindness in many homes:

In the esteem of the world, they pass for kind and indulgent, whom I call cruel parents; who permit their children to get habits which they know must be afterwards broken. Nay, some are so stupidly fond, as in sport to teach their children to do things, which in a while after they have severely beaten them for doing. When a child is corrected it must be conquered, and this will be no hard matter to do, if it be not grown headstrong by too much indulgence. And when the will of a child is totally subdued, and it is brought to revere and stand in awe of the parents, then a great many childish follies and inadvertences may be passed by. Some should be overlooked and taken no notice of, and others mildly reproved; but no wilful transgression ought ever to be forgiven children, without chastisement, less or more, as the nature and circumstances of the offence may require. I insist upon conquering the will of children betimes, because this is the only strong and rational foundation of a religious education, without which both precept and example will be ineffectual. But when this is thoroughly done, then a child is capable of being governed by the reason and piety of its parents, till its own understanding comes to maturity, and the principles of religion have taken root in the mind.[2]

Here we see some of the implications of Susanna's method. Instead of the movement being from foolish indulgence to possibly disproportionate severity, when the parent finally loses patience with a wayward child and 'puts his foot down', the tendency is reversed. Strictness comes first, to reduce the child to a normal temper of obedience, then relaxation and a more easy-going relaxationship. For all that, Susanna's insistence on 'conquering the will of children betimes' may

[1] Headingley MSS, A. f. 73.
[2] Clarke, *Wesley Family*, II, 11.

well carry obnoxious overtones for the modern ear. The question is, what did Susanna mean by the expression? She seems here to have been influenced by the educational theory of John Locke, whose works she read and admired. Charles Wesley, in dealing with the upbringing of his own first child, John, suggests a link between Susanna's determination to 'conquer the will' and Locke's similar ideas. Writing to his wife, Sally, Charles urges her confidently, 'The most important of all Locke's rules you will not forget: it is that in which the whole *secret* of education consists— make it your invariable rule to *cross his will*, in some one instance at least, every day of your life. The Lord give you wisdom and resolution to do so.'[1]

Susanna adopted a similar policy, and it may easily be made to sound harsh and inhuman. Yet by the conquest of the will Susanna surely did not mean that the parent should try systematically to break a child's will-power until it was cowed into abject submission. Her detailed exposition of her system, and the fact that her children grew into such independent and spirited men and women, are sufficient to refute any such view. It has been well said that, 'The strongest advocate of the Montessori System would hesitate to affirm that the Methodist Revival was the work of men who had been brow-beaten and cowed in their infancy.'[2] Susanna's stress upon 'conquering' or 'subduing' the child's will meant something other than that. It seems to have meant primarily a refusal to let the child have its own way in everything. Here surely is the issue which at an astonishingly early age confronts every parent: is the will of the child, freakish and undisciplined as it is, to be allowed to govern its life and conduct? If it is, then the 'spoiled' child is the result, whose marred, misshapen nature makes clear that in getting the better of its parents, it has got the worst of itself.

[1] Cited in F. Baker, *Charles Wesley as Revealed by his Letters*, p. 109.
[2] M. R. Brailsford, *Susanna Wesley, the Mother of Methodism*, p. 55.

That, to Susanna, as a wise parent, was sheer cruelty to
the child, who could afterwards be brought to disciplined
goodness only by a fierce and painful struggle. Her alternative was simply that the child's will should be governed,
trained and guided according to the enlightened will of a
godly parent. It is vital to realize that it is *self-will* which
Susanna is anxious to subdue. The final paragraph of her
exposition of this theme reads:

I cannot yet dismiss this subject. As self-will is the root of all sin
and misery, so whatever cherishes this in children insures their
after wretchedness and irreligion; whatever checks and mortifies
it promotes their future happiness and piety. This is still more
evident if we farther consider that religion is nothing else than the
doing the *will of God*, and not our own; that the one grand im-
pediment to our temporal and eternal happiness being this *self-
will*, no indulgences of it can be trivial, no denial unprofitable.
Heaven or hell depends on this alone. So that the parent who
studies to subdue it in his child, works together with God in the
renewing and saving a soul. The parent who indulges it does the
devil's work; makes religion impracticable, salvation unattain-
able, and does all that in him lies to damn his child soul and
body, for ever.[1]

Strong words! But they spring from and are consistent with
a whole carefully thought-out scheme of theology and
devotion, which at a later point we must examine in detail.[2]

The modern parent who is self-indulgent and ill-disci-
plined, may well look askance at Susanna's approach, and
prefer for his children the easier option of 'self-expression'
and 'free development'. He will have noted with disapproval
that her 'method' not only sets a high standard for children,
but makes very great demands on *parents*. It is not a matter
of the parent imposing his will on the child, but rather of
those who are consciously trying to live in conformity to the
divine will, bringing up their children in the same obedience.
Dr John Baillie, in recalling his own upbringing, has written

[1] Clarke, *Wesley Family*, II, 12.
[2] See below, pp. 131ff.

some apt words on the subject. He knew himself, from his earliest years, under the authority of the elder members of the household, and yet, he recalls,

> my earliest memories contain the knowledge that these elders did but transmit and administer an authority of which they were not themselves the ultimate source. For I never supposed that it was merely a case of my father's or mother's will being pitted against my will, still less of their power being pitted against my weakness. I knew they had a *right* to ask of me what they did and that I had no right to refuse what they asked; that is, I knew that what they desired of me was right and that my own contrary desire was wrong. But I knew also that their desiring it did not make it right, but that they desired it because it was already right independently of their desire. In other words, I understood that my parents were under the same constraint that they were so diligent in transmitting to me . . .

He concludes with a reference to his father: 'Actually, the way he himself lived, and the kind of being he was, exercised over me a more powerful and lasting constraint than all his spoken words of command.'[1] The little Wesleys knew that same constraint, and supremely from Susanna's life and character.

Constraint there certainly was in the Epworth household, but not a trace of overbearing tyranny, which had no discernible place in Susanna's character. She could be firm and strict, but her temper was even and her patience inexhaustible. Once Samuel, whose patience was as short as his temper, was amazed to hear his wife repeat the same thing twenty times to the child whom she was teaching. ' "I wonder at your patience," said he; "you have told that child twenty times that same thing." "If I had satisfied myself by mentioning it only nineteen times," she answered, "I should have lost all my labour. It was the twentieth time that crowned it." '[2] One has the impression that long before that stage, if Samuel had been doing the teaching, he would

[1] John Baillie, *Invitation to Pilgrimage*, p. 37f.
[2] Cit. Eliza Clarke, *Susanna Wesley*, p. 28.

either have given the child a good shaking, or flung away from the lesson in disgust. Again, Susanna was not a kill-joy, and games and play found a place in her children's lives as they had done in her own.[1] It was indeed a carefully regulated place, for the whole Puritan ethos, with its stress upon seriousness and duty and redeeming the time, discouraged any undue stress upon amusement and frivolity. Timothy Rogers, preaching at her sister Elizabeth's funeral, and sketching the ideal 'Character of a Good Woman', included a note on the Good Woman's upbringing of her children. Since Elizabeth Annesley is meant to exemplify this ideal, and since she resembled Susanna in character and outlook, it is interesting to compare this description with Susanna's scheme of religious education in the rectory. The Puritan family likeness is striking. In bringing up her children, says Rogers, the 'Good Woman'

forms their Minds to what is best; teaching them betimes to love God and Goodness, and to look upon Lying and Pride, and all other sins, as much below their Excellent Nature, and a Shame and a Reproach. She betimes guards them against self-will, and peevishness, and obstinacy, and the too great Love of Play, which is the common fault of these little creatures. She keeps them to work, and yet while she saves them from being idle, she is not too severe; but her Wisdom teaches her to know that such as are ingenious are more excited by good Words than by the Rod. She knows whilst their Fingers are employ'd, their Thoughts are at leisure; and therefore she orders some to read, while others sowe; and when she is discoursing, suggests to them some useful Saying or other almost at every stitch . . .[2]

Susanna also kept a balance, and was not 'too severe' with her children. She could condemn Thomas à Kempis as 'an honest, weak man', because he counselled the rejection of all amusement as sinful. There was laughter in the rectory, and there were games, including, to John's later embarrassment, games of cards. All of which helps to explain why

[1] See above, p. 55f.
[2] Rogers, *Character of a Good Woman*, p. 24f.

the Wesley children were not repelled by their early training, either as children or in later life. The fact that John Wesley sought his mother's detailed account of her educational aims and practice, is clear evidence that he, at least, was not alienated by her 'method'. Indeed, we have evidence of his positive appreciation of his mother's training, in his own writings on religious education. In his sermon, 'On Family Religion', he expounds Joshua 24. 15, 'as for me and my house, we will serve the Lord,' and urges,

Your children, while they are young, you may restrain from evil, not only by advice, persuasion, and reproof, but also by correction; only remembering, that this means is to be used last;—not till all other have been tried, and found to be ineffectual. And even then you should take the utmost care to avoid the very appearance of passion. Whatever is done should be done with mildness; nay, indeed, with kindness too. Otherwise your own spirit will suffer loss, and the child will reap little advantage.[1]

The importance which Wesley attached to the work of instructing children in the faith, is apparent from his injunctions to his preachers in the *Large Minutes* of 1789:

(1) Where there are ten children in a society, meet them at least an hour every week.
(2) Talk with them every time you see any at home.
(3) Pray in earnest for them.
(4) Diligently instruct and vehemently exhort all parents at their own houses.
(5) Preach expressly on education, particularly at Midsummer, when you speak of Kingswood.
"But I have no gift for this." Gift or no gift, you are to do it; else you are not called to be a Methodist Preacher. Do it as you can, till you can do it as you would. Pray earnestly for the gift and use the means for it.[2]

But the most interesting and relevant document for Wesley's views on the upbringing of children, is an article he wrote for the *Arminian Magazine* of 1783, entitled 'A Thought on the manner of Educating Children'. It arose, he tells his

[1] Wesley, *Works*, VII, 80.
[2] Ibid., VIII, 316. For the less attractive side of Wesley's educational theory, see his *A Token for Children*, and the Rules of Kingswood School.

readers, from a chance conversation he had with a certain gentleman who 'objected strongly to the bringing them up too strictly, to the giving them more of Religion than they liked; to the telling them of it too often, or pressing it upon them whether they will or no', so that in later life they react against it, and turn out worse than other children. Wesley's reply began by deprecating the two extremes of severity and laxity:

if they either give children too much of their own will, or need-lessly and churlishly restrain them; if they either use no punish-ment at all, or more than is necessary, the leaning either to one extreme or the other, may frustrate all their endeavours. In the latter case, it will not be strange if Religion stink in the nostrils of those that were so educated. They will naturally look upon it as an austere, melancholy thing; and if they think it necessary to salvation, they will esteem it a necessary evil, and so put it off as long as possible.[1]

All of which is surely admirable testimony to the fact that Wesley came to experience what the 1780 hymn book calls 'The Pleasantness of Religion', because of and not despite, his own upbringing. He concluded, strongly in line with his mother's teaching, that the aim of religious education was 'to turn the bias [i.e. of human nature] from Self-will, Pride, Anger, Revenge, and the Love of the World, to Resignation, Lowliness, Meekness, and the Love of God'. As far as possible, this end should be effected 'by mildness, softness and gentleness', but where necessary 'we must correct with kind severity'.[2] 'Kind severity' might serve as a good description of Susanna's own practice, and we are reminded of her by John's view that punishment should be carefully controlled and used only as a last resort. Where had Wesley, himself a childless man, learned these lessons, if not among his own brothers and sisters at Epworth, and in mature reflection on his experiences there?

[1] *Arminian Magazine* (1783), VI, 38off.
[2] Ibid.

The influence of his mother which we can detect in John's sermons and tracts, is also apparent in Charles Wesley's hymns 'For Parents' and 'For Children'. The sense of children being a solemn trust to parents, and the need to 'break the will' alike appear in the first hymn in the section 'For Parents' in the 1780 book:

> Father of all, by whom we are,
> For whom was made whatever is;
> Who hast entrusted to our care
> A candidate for glorious bliss:
>
> Poor worms of earth, for help we cry,
> For grace to guide what grace has given;
> We ask for wisdom from on high,
> To train our infant up for heaven.

In a later verse of the hymn, parents ask for grace:

> To time our every smile or frown,
> To mark the bounds of good and ill:
> And beat the pride of nature down,
> And bend or break his rising will.[1]

In another hymn we find the same emphasis on mildness and gentleness in dealing with the child, as in the writings of Susanna and of John:

> We would persuade their hearts to obey;
> With mildest zeal proceed;
> And never take the harsher way,
> When love will do the deed.
>
> For this we ask, in faith sincere,
> The wisdom from above,
> To touch their hearts with filial fear,
> And pure, ingenuous love.
>
> To watch their will, to sense inclined;
> Withhold their hurtful food;
> And gently bend their tender mind,
> And draw their souls to God.[2]

[1] *A Collection of Hymns for the use of the People called Methodists* (1780), No. 467 verses 1, 2, 8.

[2] Ibid., No. 468, verses 6, 7, 8. Cf. Hymn 469, verses 6, 12.

Finally, in a hymn 'For Children', parents beseech all the resources of the Godhead to equip them for their great task:

> Come, Father, Son, and Holy Ghost,
> To whom we for our children cry;
> The good desired and wanted most,
> Out of thy richest grace supply;
> The sacred discipline be given,
> To train and bring them up for heaven.[1]

This prayer for 'sacred discipline' was one which Susanna might well have offered. In her own way, she did so; and it was because her prayer was answered that her sons could echo so faithfully her own ideal of religious training.

Susanna's whole scheme of general education for her children was set within the framework of worship and family devotion. As she described it to John in her long letter of 1732:

Our children were taught, as soon as they could speak, the Lord's prayer, which they were made to say at rising and bed-time constantly; to which, as they grew bigger, were added a short prayer for their parents, and some collects, and some portion of Scripture, as their memories could bear. They were very early made to distinguish the Sabbath from other days, before they could well speak or go. They were as soon taught to be still at family prayers, and to ask a blessing immediately after, which they used to do by signs, before they could kneel or speak.[2]

Later, as the children grew older, Susanna set aside special times for their individual spiritual nurture: 'On Monday, I talk with Molly; on Tuesday, with Hetty; Wednesday, with Nancy; Thursday, with Jacky; Friday, with Patty; Saturday, with Charles; and with Emily and Sukey together, on Sunday.'[3] These private sessions with their mother must have left an ineffaceable impression on the minds of the children. The mere fact that she, who never trifled with one precious moment of her time, should be prepared to lay out

[1] Ibid., No. 473, verse 1.
[2] Clarke, *Wesley Family*, II, 12.
[3] Ibid., II, 92.

so much of it on their behalf, was enough of itself to convince them of the importance of the instruction they received.

The Puritan preachers of the seventeenth century had 'particularized' in their preaching, or in other words had made close and searching *personal* application of the truths of the Gospel to the condition of their hearers. Susanna stood in that tradition, as she strove with patient insight to bring home to each individual child the relevance of Christian truth to its own heart and life. Jacky (John) Wesley certainly never forgot his Thursday evening appointments with his mother. The effect of them may be gauged from a letter he wrote to her years later, when he was a Fellow of Lincoln College, Oxford. He sought her prayers to help his efforts to follow a strict rule of life and to 'renounce the world', and reminded her: 'In many things you have interceded for me and prevailed. Who knows but in this too you may be successful? If you can spare me only that little part of Thursday evening which you formerly bestowed upon me in another manner, I doubt not but it would be as useful now for correcting my heart as it was then for forming my judgement.'[1]

In addition to these personal interviews with her children, Susanna prepared for their instruction special manuals of Christian teaching. The first was composed in the form of a letter to Sukey, who was then away from home because of the fire, and expounded the Apostles' Creed. Susanna wrote from Epworth on 13th January, 1710: 'Dear Suky, Since our misfortunes have separated us from each other, and we can no longer enjoy the opportunities we once had of conversing together, I can no other way discharge the duty of a parent, or comply with my inclination of doing you all the good I can, but by writing.'[2] The strongly intellectual cast of

---

[1] Wesley, *Letters*, I, 119f.

[2] Headingley MSS, C. f. 11. Clarke, *Wesley Family*, II, 38–72, prints Susanna's exposition of the Creed in full.

Susanna's piety is seen in her stated aim, 'to lay a good foundation, that you may act upon principles, and be always able to satisfy yourself, and give a reason to others of the Faith that is in you.' She went on to review the religious instruction her daughter had already received, and urged her on to deeper understanding and more faithful practice:

You have already been instructed in some of the first principles of religion: that there is one, and but one God; that in the unity of the Godhead there is three distinct persons, Father, Son, and Holy Ghost; that this God ought to be worshipped; and you have learnt some prayers, the Creed and Catechism, in which is briefly comprehended your duty towards God, yourself, and your neighbour. But, Sukey, 'tis not learning these things by rote, nor the saying a few prayers morning and evening, that will bring you to heaven; you must understand what you say, and you must practise what you know: and since knowledge is requisite in order to practise, I shall endeavour after as plain a manner as I can, to instruct you in some of those fundamental points which are most necessary to be known, and most easy to be understood; and I earnestly beseech the great Father of spirits to guide your mind into the way of truth.[1]

Susanna apparently sent a copy of this exposition to her son Samuel too, for she wrote to him on 7th April 1710: 'I have sent you a letter which I sent to your sister Sukey at Gainsborough, which I would have you read, and copy if you have time.' She was diffident about her competence to produce these theological treatises, but believed she was making good use of her time in trying to serve her children in this way. She had rather more time to spare at this period, thanks to the fire and the scattering of her family. She explained to 'Sammy': 'When I have leisure, I think I cannot be better employed than in writing something that may be useful to my children; and though I know there are abundance of good books wherein these subjects are more fully and accurately treated of than I can pretend to write,

---

[1] Headingley MSS, C. ff. 12–13.

yet I am willing to think that my children will somewhat regard what I can do for them, though the performance be mean; since they know it comes from their mother, who is perhaps more concerned for their eternal happiness than any one in the world.'[1]

In her writings, as in all else, she had a definite plan, a 'method'. She wrote down the heads of her scheme in her evening meditation for 24th May 1711, when she admonished herself, ' 'Tis necessary to observe some method in instructing and writing for your children. Go through your brief exposition on the Ten Commandments, which are a summary of the moral law. Then briefly explain the principles of revealed religion, which will make up the second letter. Subjoin by way of essay, a short discourse on the being and attributes of God.'[2] Similarly, at the end of the treatise she sent to Sukey, she projected further writings: 'I have purposely omitted many arguments for the being of God, the divine authority of the Scriptures, for the truth of revealed religion, a future judgement; and have left the last article very imperfect, because I intend to write on all these subjects for the use of my children when I have more leisure. I shall only add a few words to prepare your mind for the second part of my discourse, obedience to the laws of God, which I shall quickly send you.'[3] If she managed to complete the paper on 'the principles of revealed religion', it does not appear to have survived; but her 'short discourse on the being and attributes of God' is in print, and her exposition of the Ten Commandments, or discourse on 'Obedience to the laws of God', is available in manuscript.[4]

She did not accomplish all this writing, however, without a good deal of misgiving and self-reproach. She felt keenly that she was ill-equipped for the task, and gives several hints

---

[1] Stevenson, *Memorials of the Wesley Family*, p. 193.
[2] Headingley MSS, A. f. 69.
[3] Headingley MSS, C. f. 59.
[4] See *W.H.S. Pubns.*, No. 3 (1898), and Headingley MSS, C. ff. 61ff.

that someone close to her—almost certainly her scholarly husband—was inclined to ridicule the whole design as a waste of time. In one of her morning meditations she catalogued the 'many discouragements' she had met with in the undertaking: 'the weakness of your mind and body, it seeming unnecessary because there are aready so many excellent discourses written on those subjects, your little time, and abundance of other business, your apprehension of censure and contempt &c.' She was not to be deterred, however, by any obstacles, believing that God's grace would strengthen her, and reflecting with her usual good sense that, 'The books that have been writ on those subjects affect not you or yours; you have them not, and perhaps your children may never see them. However, if they should, it will be some time first, and what you write will not hinder them from reaping advantage by reading them, but rather prepare their minds (by accustoming them to think and learn) for further instruction.' She returns to the likelihood of her meeting contempt in her undertaking, and we seem to hear Samuel's rather testy objection to her trespassing in the field of scholarship: 'As for creature contempt, you need not trouble yourself about such things. If any will censure you for doing your duty, what is that to you? And if any one will condemn you as unlearned and of little sense, why should that affect you, when you do not pretend to learning, and you think as meanly of your own performances as any other can do?' Samuel would have to learn the lesson of Bunyan's pilgrim, that 'He that is down needs fear no fall', and that you cannot browbeat humility. Susanna concluded, 'Let those that set up for persons of learning and extraordinary sense, mind such things. You do not (or at least ought not to) pretend to what you have not; and let those that desire a reputation in the world seek ways to obtain it.'[1] There was only one person in Epworth rectory who set up for a person

[1] Headingley MSS, A. ff. 74-7.

of learning and extraordinary sense, namely the rector. He certainly sought 'a reputation in the world', and his book dedications to the royal family were intended to secure it. Susanna's writings, on the other hand, made no pretensions either to technical scholarship or to public recognition. They were a private, pious act, undertaken out of loyalty to God and her conscience, part of the unstinted care she lavished on the upbringing of her children. We may well believe that Samuel resented the invasion of his prerogative, and sensed a rival theologian in the house. Nevertheless, despite fightings without and fears within, Susanna pressed on with her scheme and brought it to fruition. Tyerman's judgement is no doubt somewhat over-enthusiastic in its praise, but it makes clear the very real merits of Susanna's writings: 'For vigorous thought, mental discipline, clearness of apprehension, logical acumen, extensive theological knowledge, purity of style, and force of utterance, Susanna Wesley has few superiors . . . She was an accomplished scholar, a learned student, a correct philosopher, and a profound divine.'[1] Much of this eulogy might be applied to John Wesley, who was his mother's aptest pupil, and part of the handsome justification of all her efforts as an amateur theologian.

Her influence over her children, through her life and teaching, was powerful and lasting. When the boys left home for school and university, she was their faithful correspondent and mentor. In return, they as grown men still valued her advice, and sought it equally on theological questions, matters of conduct, and problems of the spiritual life. On 5th May 1729, Charles, who was then screwing himself up for the spiritual athleticism of the Holy Club, wrote to John: 'I won't give myself *leisure* to relapse, for I'm assured, if I have no business of my own, the Devil will soon find me some. You may show this if you think proper to my mother,

[1] L. Tyerman, *Life and Times of the Rev. Samuel Wesley*, p. 125.

for I would gladly have a letter from her upon this subject.'[1] A few years later, as they were both contemplating going to Georgia as missionaries, they first laid the whole project before their mother, to obtain her full approval and consent. John especially would continue to consult his mother on matters of moment, whether personal or doctrinal, to the end of her life. Her resolve to be 'more particularly careful of the soul of this child', was so fully kept that the child, become a man and leader of men, was more particularly careful to ascertain her mind before taking major decisions. Julia Wedgwood's study of Wesley draws attention to his correspondence with his mother as evidence against the view that would write him down as a proud and domineering character. Susanna's letters, she contends, could not have been written to a son who was not singularly ready to be taught. 'To how few clever young men of twenty-three could a mother say, with no softening expression of doubt, "You are somewhat mistaken in your opinion of"—anything that was as open to his investigation as to hers. Many faults are compatible with this submissiveness of intellect; some perhaps are even connected with it. But that impatience for dominion which has been ascribed to John Wesley assuredly belongs to neither class.'[2]

Susanna was a good mother to her children, in the sense that she cared deeply for their physical and moral welfare; but she was far more to them than that. She laid herself out unstintingly for their souls' good: she was to them teacher, pastor, class leader, and an outstanding example of godly life. The words of the memorial tablet to John Wesley in Epworth Methodist Church, may be widened in their reference to embrace all the Wesley children. After recording John's birth at Epworth and naming his parents, it seizes

---

[1] F. Baker, *Charles Wesley as Revealed by his Letters*, p. 13.
[2] Julia Wedgwood, *John Wesley and the Evangelical Reaction of the Eighteenth Century* (1870), p. 37f.

upon the salient fact that by them, 'he was prayerfully educated in the things of God.' In that prayerful education of the Wesleys, there seems small doubt that Susanna bore the major and decisive part.

CHAPTER FIVE

Serious Godliness

It is only serious godliness that can really abate the
vanity that cleaves to every condition. *Samuel
Annesley*

*T*HE *Oxford Dictionary of the Christian Church*
describes St Teresa of Avila as 'a woman of strong character,
shrewdness, and great practical ability', and adds that 'Her
combination of mystic experience with ceaseless activity as a
reformer and organizer make her life the classical instance
for those who contend that the highest contemplation is not
incompatible with great practical achievements'. The tribute
is striking, and might with little alteration be applied to
Susanna, who, like St Teresa, united the monastic strictness
of a devotional rule with a superbly efficient discharge of
practical duties. Her biographers have often noted that her
rule of life had a certain affinity with that of a religious order:
her ordered timetable for the household, her exclusive concentration on her home and family which virtually immured
her from the world, her overriding religious purpose,—all
these challenge the comparison. Mrs Harrison speaks of 'her

glorious method and routine of the cloister';[1] John Kirk speaks of her living 'a sort of cloister-life';[2] and Susanna herself gives warrant for this monastic analogy, when she states that only a mother who is prepared to renounce the world can possibly carry through her educational programme.

We see in Susanna a remarkable blend of the active and the contemplative life. Yet despite the comparisons cited, the inspiration behind her ordered religious life was not monastic. Her life exemplified rather Luther's teaching on the calling of the Christian woman. Luther had taught that the saint's path to heaven was to be trodden, not by renouncing the offices of wife and mother, but precisely through fulfilling them, while at the same time making the concerns of the spirit paramount. Such teaching of the Reformation was mediated to Susanna through the Puritan tradition in which she was reared. Indeed, it is in her devotional life and practice that her Puritan heritage and upbringing are most clearly apparent. In her writings all the great Puritan keywords recur: method, discipline, duty, reason, conscience, experience, and holiness. These terms, which give the clue to her whole pattern of life, were translated into an ordered framework of Puritan theology and devotion.

The tone of Puritan devotion is set by Milton's desire to live, 'As ever in my great Task-master's eye.' The Puritan was acutely conscious that the whole of his life was lived *coram Deo*, in the holy presence of the all-seeing God. Susanna's father gave eloquent expression to this insight in one of his sermons. Preaching from Acts 24. 16, on the theme 'How may we be universally and exactly conscientious?' he urged his hearers to 'daily actual repentance', and added: 'Compose thy self to live as under God's eye, live as in the more than sensible presence of the Jealous God. Remember,

[1] G. Elsie Harrison, *Son to Susanna*, p. 24.
[2] John Kirk, *The Mother of the Wesleys*, p. 256.

all things are naked and bare before him, you cannot deceive him, for he is infinite wisdom; you cannot fly from him for he is everywhere; you cannot bribe him, for he is righteousness itself.'[1] The same emphasis occurs frequently in Susanna's own writings. In 1710, her schoolboy son Samuel wrote from Westminster, complaining that he was 'as unstable as water' in his efforts to live the Christian life, and seeking her advice and help. Her first instruction was: 'Endeavour to get as deep an impression on your mind as is possible, of the awful and constant presence of the great and holy God. Consider frequently, that wherever you are, or whatever you are about, he always adverts to your thoughts and actions, in order to a future retribution. He is about our beds, and about our paths, and spies out all our ways; and whenever you are tempted to the commission of any sin, or the omission of any duty, make a pause, and say to yourself,—What am I about to do? God sees me!'[2]

What she preached to her children, she practised herself. In one of her morning meditations she reminded herself: 'Religion is not to be confined to the church, or closet, nor exercised only in prayer and mediation. Everywhere we are in the presence of God, and every word and action is capable of morality.'[3] Not many months after her letter to young Samuel, on 21st April 1711, she wrote for her own benefit the same advice. She had been meditating on the need to be scrupulously truthful in recounting actions and events, 'lest your invention supply the defect of your memory, ever remembering you are in the presence of the great and holy God. Every sin is a contradiction and offence to some divine attribute. Lying is opposite and offensive to the truth of God.'[4] On another occasion she urged herself, 'Be careful to . . . maintain a constant habitual sense of God in your

[1] *The Morning-Exercise at Cripplegate*, ed. Annesley, p. 19 (2).
[2] Clarke, *Wesley Family*, II, 145f.
[3] *Wesley Banner* (1852), IV, 201.
[4] Headingley MSS, A. f. 28.

mind. Live and act as in his presence; think often of his omnipresence and omniscience; of his power, wisdom, goodness, justice, truth, &c., and above all, of his infinite purity, which will be a check upon the mind, and be the best preservative against all temptations.'[1]

These extracts may suggest that living in the great Taskmaster's eye was a grim business. It would seem that God's omnipresence was interpreted far more as jealous oversight than guardian care. It was indeed a God-*fearing* form of piety, which bred a deep reverence for the divine holiness. Yet, more fundamental than reverent fear was the supreme motive of love to God. Dr Annesley had taught that love to God was the mainspring of all Christian living: 'Do all you do out of love to God. Spiritual love-sickness is the soul's healthfullest condition. When love to God is both cause, means, motive and end of all our activity in the business of Religion, then the soul is upon the wing towards its rest. Then is our love to other things regular, when the alone goodness of God moves us to love them.'[2] Susanna echoes her father with impressive frequency at this point. She reasons sternly with herself that, 'To apprehend God displeased . . . and yet to be capable of relishing the childish amusements of the world is an argument of a vain and irreligious mind. That person that truly loves God above all things . . . is as incapable of rest, or satisfaction of mind, under a sense of his anger, as his body would be at ease when labouring under an acute distemper. If, therefore, this be your case, be assured you do not love God as you ought to do.'[3] Next day, with money troubles pressing upon her, she urges herself: 'Learn by practice to love God above all things, and you will be out of the power of the world, and then to be without wealth will give no uneasiness.'[4] Elsewhere she meditates: 'We must love the

[1] Headingley MSS, A. f. 34.
[2] *The Morning-Exercise at Cripplegate*, ed. Annesley, p. 22.
[3] *Wesley Banner* (1852), IV, 201.
[4] Ibid., IV, 202.

Lord our God with all the heart, with all the mind, with all the soul, and with all the strength. We must love him so as to desire him, desire him so as to be uneasy without him, without his favour, without some resemblance, such as our nature, in this imperfect state, can bear, of him.'[1]

In her struggle to make the love of God central to her whole life, Susanna might have been consciously modelling herself upon her father's precepts. In a sermon on Psalm 97 : 1–2, 'The Lord reigneth; let the earth rejoice,' Dr Annesley urged: 'If a good man should be deprived of his temporal comforts, it will commend spiritual ones the more to him. God's voice is never so sweet, as when he speaks comfortably in a wilderness.' That was a truth Susanna knew experimentally, as she soldiered on in the penury of Epworth rectory, surrounded by the desolate fenland of the Isle of Axholme. Her father continued his counsel: 'Be very serious and frequent in your meditations upon God's governing the world.' Few could have been as serious and frequent as his youngest daughter. His final injunction, which might stand as the watchword of Susanna's whole devotional life, exhorted his hearers to 'perseverance in godliness', and assured them, 'You may live by faith, while you walk by rule; you may walk believingly and cheerfully, while you walk regularly.'[2] He amplified the point in a sermon on Ecclesiastes 6:11–12, arguing that it is only 'serious godliness' which 'sweetens all the bitterness of a poor condition, bears up the heart under all those difficulties that were otherwise intolerable; GOD makes up their worldly poverty with riches of grace.' Therefore, he advised his hearers, 'Make conscience of both sorts of duties, religious and worldly; and allot fit and distinct times for heavenly and worldly business; but with this difference, let religion mix itself with worldly business, and

---

[1] Headingley MSS, A.f. 26. For the same motif in Wesley, see M. Schmidt, *John Wesley: A Theological Biography*, I, 116.
[2] *Christian Library*, ed. Wesley, XXIV, 37f., 39f.

spare not; but let not the world break in upon religion.'[1]

The framework of Susanna's piety was that of Puritan Method. It involved a carefully ordered timetable, so that she could scrupulously fulfil all her household and teaching duties, and at the same time make allowance for her more specifically religious exercises. Of course her household tasks were not undertaken as mere chores, but as themselves in their measure religious acts. Yet the steady ardour which she brought to her domestic duties depended for its source and kindling upon her withdrawal from her family for private devotion, for an hour both morning and evening, with a briefer break at noon. The effect on her children of their mother's punctual withdrawals from the busy life of the household can well be imagined. They divined, as John's mature testimony shows, that here was the source of her poise and serenity, her unruffled control of all the pressing business of the day.

The cast of her piety has been described by Dr Martin Schmidt as an 'intellectualist and voluntary mysticism'. Certainly her emphasis on the will, on humility, and on the outworking of prayer in love to neighbour, are all strongly reminiscent of the mysticism of St Teresa and *The Interior Castle*. There is no evidence that Susanna came directly under the influence of Teresa's writings, though these were known to Dr Annesley, who referred in a sermon to 'Teresia's Maxim, "All that is not God is nothing" '.[2] What is certain is that another Roman Catholic work, Lorenzo Scupoli's *Pugna Spiritualis* or *Spiritual Conflict*, held a central place in her devotion. Written by an Italian monk of the Theatine Order, this book had become known in England through a Spanish translation by Juan de Castaniza.[3] Its message centred round the call to Christian perfection, and it called

[1] *Christian Library*, ed. Wesley, XXIV, 428f., 451.

[2] *A Supplement to the Morning-Exercise at Cripplegate*, ed. Annesley (1676), p. 26.

[3] The *Spiritual Conflict* was published in English in a modern edition, under the title of *Unseen Warfare*, by E. Kadloubovski and G. E. H. Palmer (1952).

upon man, in the words of Dr Schmidt, to 'hate himself, renounce his own Ego, and turn with whole-hearted love to God. It is not feeling but the understanding and the will which are addressed in the first place; hence this is primarily an intellectualist and voluntary mysticism, even if the emotional element follows'.[1] The essential factor in Christian obedience, according to the *Spiritual Conflict*, was the *virtus patientiae*, the readiness to suffer. It involved a willingness to accept awkward people and unpleasant circumstances as all grist to the mill of perfection.

At this point in Susanna's devotion, however, in her striving after Christian perfection, it is possible to trace a more direct and homely influence upon her, in the teaching and practice of her father. Dr Annesley's life was marked by a constant struggle to submit himself to the divine will, such as is enjoined by the *Spiritual Conflict*. Significantly, Daniel Williams stressed this aspect of his friend's Christian life in the funeral sermon he preached on Dr Annesley: 'He obeyed God's will as he had notice of it, and whatever labour, expense, or danger attended it. This will of God he still (i.e. always) consulted, as to the matter and manner of his performances.'[2] Annesley himself came close to the spirit of the *Spiritual Conflict*, when he defined the meaning of 'serious godliness' as 'to hate sin, and love holiness, to live a life of faith, in dependence upon God, and resignation to him; to live above the transports of hopes and fears about things temporal; and to grow up in the graces and comforts of the HOLY GHOST, for things eternal'.[3] It is possible, then, that Susanna was in a measure predisposed towards the *Spiritual Conflict* by her father's typically Puritan conception of the Christian life as a Holy War.

Yet her devotion was never exclusively dominated by the

[1] M. Schmidt, *John Wesley: A Theological Biography*, I, 48f.

[2] D. Williams, *The Excellency of a Publick Spirit*, p. 5.

[3] *Christian Library*, ed. Wesley, XXIV, 425. For this same theme in Susanna's writings, see *Wesley Banner*, IV, 286, 324.

Spiritual Conflict, nor by any one book of personal piety. She was deliberately eclectic in her approach, and ranged in her reading from à Kempis to Samuel Clark the Deist. Of the Anglican divines she read Bishop Beveridge and Dr Rust, as well as Henry More and John Norris ('Dr More' and 'Mr Norris'), the Cambridge Platonists. Pascal she quotes both in her theological writings and her private correspondence. A letter she wrote to John and Charles in 1732 gives an interesting glimpse of her theological reading, and shows her independent turn of mind:

'The Life of God in the Soul of Man', is an excellent good book, and was an acquaintance of mine many years ago; but I have unfortunately lost it. There are many good things in Castaniza; more in Baxter; yet are neither without faults, which I overlook for the sake of their virtues. Nor can I say, of all the books of divinity I have read, which is the best; one is best at one time, one at another, according to the temper and disposition of the mind.[1]

Henry Scougal (1650–78) was a distinguished Scottish Episcopalian, whose classic *Life of God in the Soul of Man* was first published in 1677. Susanna's brief survey of her reading thus brings together a Scottish Episcopalian, an Italian Roman Catholic (Scupoli in Castaniza's translation), and an English Puritan, Baxter.

It is interesting that Susanna rates the writings of Richard Baxter so highly. She does not specify any of his works, but her sister Elizabeth knew and loved his *Saints' Everlasting Rest*. Timothy Rogers, preaching her funeral sermon, recalled that Elizabeth had found the book congenial reading in her last illness: 'Mr Baxter's *Saints' Rest* was a book in which she took a great delight; there is a spirit of such seriousness and heavenliness in that book, that all the while one reads, one seems to be in heaven.'[2] Given the common background of

---

[1] Clarke, *Wesley Family*, II, 103. For John Wesley's similarly eclectic approach, see *Christian Library*, I, ix (Preface).

[2] T. Rogers, *Character of a Good Woman*, p. 129.

Susanna and her sister, and their similarity in character and piety, it is likely that Susanna knew the *Saints' Rest* too. Certainly it chimes in with the spirit of her own devotion, and being written out of Baxter's sickness it would speak to her own condition. It evidently spoke to her son's too, for Wesley published an abridged version of Baxter's classic, together with Scougal's *Life of God*, in his *Christian Library*.

All of Susanna's life and activities were undergirded by the means of grace, which included not only the spiritual reading we have surveyed, but also meditation, prayer, self-examination and Holy Communion. Her father had preached on the need for 'serious meditation' and besought his congregation to give the 'good things' of their reading 'a little heart-room, bestow second-thoughts upon them, shut the book when you have read a little, and think of it, and it will abide'.[1] In the Puritan circles in which Susanna was reared, meditation was a hallmark of all serious piety. Dr Thomas Manton, a friend of her father, preached from Matthew 15: 7–8, on 'How may we cure distractions in holy duties?' and argued that one way was to mingle with 'the offices of the common life' what he called 'gracious meditations and short ejaculations'. Moreover, 'frequent solemn meditation' helped to curb distractions in the spiritual life: 'If the understanding were oftener taken up with the things of God, and our thoughts were kept in more frequent exercise, they would the better come to hand . . . he that hath stocked his heart with holy thoughts will not find carnal musings so rife and frequent.'[2] Similarly Richard Baxter assumed that 'most serious' and 'affectionate Meditations'[3] were a normal part of the Christian life.

Puritan piety was earnest, reflective, and systematic, as its emphasis upon meditation suggests. The Puritan coveted the

[1] *Christian Library*, ed. Wesley, XXIV, 49f.
[2] *The Morning-Exercise at Cripplegate*, ed. Annesley, p. 477.
[3] Baxter, *The Divine Life* (1664), pp. 171, 173. See also Baxter, *The Saints' Everlasting Rest, Practical Works*, ed. Orme, XXIII, 310ff.

tribute paid to Baxter at his funeral: 'In him the Vertues of
the Contemplative and Active Life were eminently united.
His time was spent in Communion with God, and in Charity
to Men.'[1] Meditation not only refined and strengthened the
soul, but led to increased effectiveness in Christian service.
Dr Annesley expounded in his preaching the need for daily
meditation, and urged his hearers:

Did you but once a day . . . solemnly place your selves in God's
presence; beg of him the fixing and flowing of your thoughts, that
your thoughts might be graciously fix'd, yet as graciously en-
larg'd; let the subject matter of them be something Spiritual;
endeavour to fill your heads, and affect your hearts with holy
musings, till you come to some resolution, which resolution close
with Prayer, and follow with endeavours; O how would this
(even e're you are aware) engage your Souls to love God.[2]

He went on to show the need to 'methodize' one's meditations, 'to tye your thoughts together, and so fasten them that
they may not be lost, that your musing time may not be
reckon'd among your lost time.' One way of tying the
thoughts together and of preventing meditation from becoming mere day-dreaming, was to follow the practice of keeping
a spiritual journal—'the Puritan confessional',[3] as Professor
Haller aptly calls it. Susanna kept just such a journal, and
carefully recorded in it the substance of her meditations and
the vows or resolutions which flowed from them. Both she
and her sister Elizabeth evidently took most seriously this
whole aspect of their father's piety. The Puritan minister
who preached Elizabeth's funeral sermon praised her as the
exemplar of 'The Character of a Good Woman', whose
'first Visit is to Heaven, and she smells of it all the day.
In her Closet she pleases her self with sweet and serious
Meditations, and for these she fetches Matter from the Holy
Scriptures; which she diligently reads, and which she dearly

---

[1] Wm. Bates, *A Funeral-Sermon for . . . Mr Richard Baxter* (1692), p. 114.
[2] *A Supplement to the Morning-Exercise at Cripplegate*, ed. Annesley, p. 19.
[3] W. Haller, *The Rise of Puritanism* (1938), p. 97.

loves above all other Books'.[1] Susanna's practice was similar,
and the high place she assigned to meditation is clear from
a letter to John, in which she comments: 'I see nothing in
the disposition of your time but what I approve, unless it be
that you do not assign enough of it to meditation; which is,
I conceive, incomparably the best means to spiritualize our
affections, confirm our judgement, and add strength to our
pious resolutions, of any exercise whatever.'[2]

For Susanna, meditation led naturally into self-examination, and she addressed herself in the second person as she
reviewed her thoughts, words and actions in a detailed and
clinical scrutiny. A typical noontide meditation runs: 'It is
necessary for you, if you would preserve your liberty, and
live free from sin, to mortify your appetites, for if they
remain in power, restrain them as you will, or can, still some
circumstances or seasons will occur, wherein they will betray
you, and compel you to act contrary to your better judgement.'[3] Here again Susanna was the true daughter of her
Puritan father. Dr Annesley's sermons stressed the vital
importance of self-examination, and as one recipe for a good
conscience he advised his congregation, 'Be serious and frequent in the examination of your heart and life. This is so
necessary to the getting & keeping of a right & peaceable
Conscience, that 'tis impossible to have either without it.'
He lamented 'the carelessness of most, that are better
acquainted with any thing than themselves', and asked,
with all the existential urgency of Puritan preaching, 'Who
questions with his own heart, Who am I? What do I? How
live I? Is the course I follow good and lawful? Is that which
I omit my duty, or not? Is God my friend? Am I his? What
hope have I of heaven? Say I die tomorrow, today, this very
hour, where is my assurance I shall be saved?'

[1] T. Rogers, *The Character of a Good Woman*, p. 13.
[2] Quoted by J. Kirk, *Mother of the Wesleys*, p. 248.
[3] *The Morning-Exercise at Cripplegate*, ed. Annesley, p. 20f.

Annesley held that careful self-examination should be made daily, both morning and evening, the Christian viewing the day first in prospect and then in retrospect: 'Every evening ere you sleep, review your carriage in the day, what you have done, or spoke, or thought, that is but so much as indecent (i.e. unbecoming). Whether your hearts have been intent upon religion, and indifferent to the world. Briefly, have special care of two portions of your time, viz. morning and evening, the morning to fore-think what ought to be done, and the evening to examine whether you have done what you ought.'[1] Susanna's practice was fully in line with her father's teaching, and in one of her meditations she admonished herself, 'Keep the mind in a temper for recollection, and often in the day call it in from outward objects, lest it wander into forbidden paths. Make an examination of your conscience at least three times a day, and omit no opportunity of retirement from the world.'[2]

This aspect of Puritan piety, centring upon meditation and self-examination, led to an inner dialogue, a communing of the soul with itself and with God. Professor Talon traces the development of Bunyan's vivid dialogue to this hidden source, and comments: 'The dialogue-form with questions and answers is a repetition of the inner monologue which is often nothing more than an implicit dialogue.'[3] Yet where Talon thinks in terms of a 'self-with-self dialogue', P. T. Forsyth, writing on prayer from within this same tradition of Puritan devotion, suggests a deeper understanding of the dialogue as 'the dialogue of grace' which 'is really the monologue of the divine nature in self-communing

---

[1] *The Morning-Exercise at Cripplegate*, ed. Annesley, p. 20f.

[2] Headingley MSS, A. f. 31. For the rigorous system of self-examination adopted by Wesley and his associates in the Holy Club, see M. Schmidt, *John Wesley, A Theological Biography*, I, 97ff. Dr Schmidt, significantly, sees the Holy Club scheme as 'an example of the way in which the Puritan practices of self-control and self-criticism have been intensified and formulated into an extraordinarily exacting oversight of the individual's affairs'.

[3] H. Talon, *John Bunyan, the Man and his Work*, p. 128.

love'.[1] The communion with God which was characterized by such stringent self-examination was one source of the profound psychological insight of the Puritan divines. There is a notable example of this insight in the section of Baxter's *Autobiography* entitled by his modern editor *Richard Baxter's Self-Analysis and Life-Review*.[2] A good example of this Puritan insight is the conception of the 'darling sin', which occurs also in Susanna's writings and in John Wesley. Thomas Doolittle, preaching at Cripplegate in 1661, warned that only when a man was willing to give up 'his bosom sin, his darling' was he truly sincere. Otherwise his Achilles' heel would prove fatal: 'one stab at the heart with a pen-knife, will as certainly kill a man, as a thousand wounds with a sword.'[3] In the same vein Dr Annesley preached, 'Come, Sirs, let me deal plainly with you; you are shameful strangers to your own heart, if you do not know which is your darling sin, or sins; and you are traitors to your own souls, if you do not endeavour a thorough mortification.'[4] Susanna, in a letter to John Wesley of 1727, carried the thought further by pointing out that it was vain to try to compensate for indulgence of a darling sin by increased rigour in other areas of one's life: 'I am verily persuaded, that the reason why so many seek to enter into the kingdom of heaven, but are not able, is, there is some Delilah, some one beloved vice, they will not part with; hoping that by a strict observance of their duty in other things, that particular fault will be dispensed with. But, alas! they miserably deceive themselves . . .'[5] Hence the need for eternal vigilance and constant self-

[1] P. T. Forsyth, *The Soul of Prayer*, p. 42.
[2] See Baxter, *Autobiography*, ed. J. M. Lloyd Thomas, pp. 103ff.
[3] *The Morning-Exercise at Cripplegate*, ed. Annesley, p. 308f.
[4] *A Supplement to the Morning-Exercise at Cripplegate*, ed. Annesley, p. 15. See also John Bunyan, *The Heavenly Footman* (1698); 'In the doctrine of mortification is also much of the cross. Is it nothing for a man to lay hands on his vile opinions, on his vile sins, on his bosom sins, on his beloved, pleasant, darling sins . . .?' (*The Works of John Bunyan*, ed. G. Offor (1854–55), III, 387.)
[5] Clarke, *Wesley Family*, II, 22.

examination. Wesley himself, in one of his translations of hymns from the German, Tersteegen's *Verborgne Gottesliebe du*, used language which echoes this strain in Puritan moral theology:

> O hide this self from me, that I
> No more, but Christ in me, may live!
> My vile affections crucify,
> Nor let *one darling lust* survive!
> In all things nothing may I see,
> Nothing desire or seek, but Thee![1]

The means of grace by which Susanna's piety was sustained included not only spiritual reading, prayer and meditation, public worship and private self-scrutiny, but also the sacrament of Holy Communion. It might be thought that at this point Susanna stepped outside the Puritan tradition in which she was reared, with its overwhelming emphasis on the majesty of the preached Word. Such an emphasis, however, in the mainstream of the Puritan tradition, by no means involved a disparagement of the sacrament. Baxter has a lyrical passage on 'the Sacrament of the Body and Blood of Christ', which combines belief in the Real Presence with stress upon the sealing of the Covenant between Christ and His Church. The central importance of the Covenant in Puritan theology highlights the significance of Baxter's statement that it is in the sacrament that the Covenant is sealed. The passage, both for its intrinsic merit, and because it brings out a side of Puritan devotion too often neglected, deserves quotation in full. In the sacrament, writes Baxter:

Christ himself with his Covenant-gifts are all delivered to us by these investing signs of his own institution; even as knighthood is given by a sword, and as a house is delivered by a key, or land by a twig and turf. Nowhere is God so near to man as in Jesus Christ; and nowhere is Christ so familiarly represented to us, as in this holy sacrament. Here we are called to sit with him at his

---

[1] *Methodist Hymn Book* (1933), Hymn 433, verse 5. My italics.

Table, as his invited welcome guests; to commemorate his sacrifice, to feed upon his very flesh and blood; that is, with our mouths upon his representative flesh and blood, and with our applying faith upon his real flesh and blood, by such a feeding as belongs to faith. The Marriage-Covenant betwixt God incarnate, and his espoused ones, is there publicly sealed, celebrated and solemnized. . . . If ever a believer may on earth expect his kindest entertainment, and near access, and a humble intimacy with his Lord, it is in the participation of this sacrifice-feast, which is called the Communion because it is appointed as well for our special communion with Christ as with one another. It is here that we have the fullest intimation, expression and communication of the wondrous love of God; and therefore it is here that we have the loudest call, and best assistance to make a large return of love. . . .[1]

He goes on to warn that there should be no 'rushing upon holy things with a presumptuous careless common frame of heart',—a warning of which Susanna, at least, had no need.

There is evidence that in her sacramental devotion Susanna stood in this high Puritan tradition, which esteemed the Lord's Supper as a sovereign means of grace. We have not to hand any writings of Dr Annesley on the sacrament, but there has survived a graphic account of his celebrating Holy Communion at his meeting-house in Little St Helen's. A visitor to the congregation describes the scene:

The Dr went all over the meeting first, to see who was there, then spake something of the Sermon, then read the words of Institution, then prayed and eat and drunk himself, then gave to every one with his own Hand, dropping pertinent Expressions. In our Pue said—Now our Spikenard should give its smell; and said to me, Remember the Death of Christ . . . The Deacon followed the Dr, and when his Cup was empty filled it again: as at our Pue all had drunk but I, he filled the Cup, and then gave it to me; said, as he gave it—Must be ready in new Obedience, and stick at nothing for Christ.[2]

The pledge of obedience and self-offering, the *sacramentum* or oath of allegiance solemnly sworn by the Christian disciple

[1] Baxter, *The Divine Life*, Pt. I, *A Treatise of the Knowledge of God* (1664), p. 174f.

[2] *Diary of Samuel Sewall*, I, 253ff., as quoted in Horton Davies, *The Worship of the English Puritans*, p. 210.

who takes the sacrament, is admirably expressed in his injunction to 'stick at nothing for Christ'; and the phrase might well stand as the watchword of his own life, and of Puritanism at its best. Here it serves to underline the fact that the Puritan ideal of Christianity in earnest included a vital attachment to the sacrament as a means of grace.

The solemnity of Holy Communion for the Puritans was marked by their careful preparation for receiving it. Timothy Rogers, in his sketch of Puritan piety based on the life of Susanna's sister, Elizabeth, made this preparation a normative element in the 'Good Woman's' devotion:

When there is a sacrament, then she dispatches all her worldly affairs with great haste and expedition; and beginning with elevations of her heart to God, tries her own ways, and examines whether she is sincere, and all her graces are in exercise; she very wisely trims her lamp, and so is fit to meet the Lord. He only knows with what rapture she longs to see his face, and to feel his love; she longs to feast with her best beloved, and to have the foretastes of heaven at his holy table.[1]

One of Elizabeth's meditations before receiving the sacrament has been preserved, and is marked by a fervent belief in the Real Presence: 'O dearest Jesus, I cannot at this sacrament take a denial of thy gracious Presence; I come to meet with God, and I cannot be contented without him; I would have all my graces flourish, I would have all sin destroy'd and rooted out . . . I did . . . in these and the like expressions, make over myself to be more entirely God's; and I dare own upon review, that I enjoyed Christ.'[2]

In this same tradition, Susanna carried out a careful self-examination before she went to the Lord's Table. Indeed, she was so rigorously conscientious that both her body and spirit were fatigued for some days after. She acutely analysed her condition in one of her meditations:

[1] Rogers, *The Character of a Good Woman*, p. 37f.
[2] Ibid., p. 147f.

You have of late often experienced that the more accurate you have been in the work of preparation for the sacrament, the more indisposed you have been to spiritual things, (especially for meditation, and reflection) for sometimes one, sometimes two, or three days after; and this hath been a great discouragement to you, and you have thought that your soul has received no benefit from that sacred ordinance. Now the reason of it I apprehend to be this—long intense thinking, keeping the mind for a considerable time to hard exercise, does necessarily impair the bodily strength, where persons are of a weak constitution, and that the mind being under the influences of the body in this imperfect state, it cannot exert itself, till that hath again recovered its vigour, which requires some time; and you may observe that as the body is refreshed, the soul is strengthened. Therefore be not discouraged; but endeavour to keep your mind as composed as possible, and pray to God to preserve you from temptation during this bodily indisposition, and that as your day is, so your strength may be. Amen, Lord Jesus![1]

It was from her own experience of the sacrament as a sovereign means of grace that she wrote to her eldest son Samuel, while he was at Westminster School: 'I am heartily glad that you have already, and that you design again to receive the Holy Sacrament; for there is nothing more proper or effectual for the strengthening and refreshing the mind, than the frequent partaking of that blessed ordinance.'[2]

The sacrament was again the subject of correspondence between mother and son in 1732, when John consulted Susanna, as his mentor and mother-confessor, about the views of one of his Oxford friends on the subject of the Real Presence. Susanna's reply shows that for her the sacrament was no mere memorial of Jesus, but a genuine encounter with Him.

The young gentleman you mention seems to me to be in the right concerning the real presence of Christ in the Sacrament.

[1] Headingley MSS, A. f. 54f.; printed in *Wesley Banner* (1852), IV, 406. See also Stevenson, *Memorials of the Wesley Family*, p. 209, for Susanna's similar advice to John.

[2] *Arminian Magazine* (1788), XI, 36. On Susanna's experience of Assurance in the sacrament, see below, p. 197f.

I own I never understood by the real presence more than what he has elegantly expressed, that 'the Divine nature of Christ is then eminently present to impart, by the operation of His Holy Spirit, the benefits of His Death to worthy receivers.' Surely the Divine presence of our Lord, thus applying the virtue and merits of the great Atonement to each true believer makes the consecrated bread more than a sign but with it the thing signified, all the benefits of His Incarnation and Passion; but still, however this Divine institution may seem to others, to me it is full of mystery.[1]

Her approval of doctrine 'elegantly expressed' is a typically eighteenth-century touch, but Susanna goes far beyond the often cold and rationalistic piety of the times in her devotion to the sacrament, as in so much else. Her stress on the operation of the Spirit in the sacrament, often echoed in Charles Wesley's *Hymns on the Lord's Supper*; her underlining of the need for 'worthy receiving'; and the characteristic reverence and humility of her last sentence, with its concern to safeguard the mystery;—all these reveal a depth and warmth of devotion, which, though expressed in the language of the eighteenth century, are much more redolent of that great though wayward age of faith, the seventeenth.

Professor Gerald Cragg's study of the changes in religious thought within the Church of England from 1660 to 1700 is suggestively entitled *From Puritanism to the Age of Reason*. The first thirty years of Susanna's life coincided with the last three decades of this period. Did she make any such transition herself? It may well be argued that she did. She was bred in Puritanism, left Nonconformity for Anglicanism, and from her own account was influenced during her formative years by the Socinian heresy. Moreover, there are numerous passages in her writings which lend colour to the view that her piety and devotion were markedly rationalistic. Reason, reasonable, rational,—these words occur as often in her writings as in those of her son John. Her letters,

[1] Wesley, *Letters*, I, 118.

meditations, and theological treatises all reveal her strong desire to hold a rational faith. More than once, indeed, she identifies natural and revealed religion, and asserts that the Gospel simply results in bringing man again under the rule of right reason. In her 'Conference' with her daughter Emilia, she writes: 'Do you think our Saviour taught any other than natural religion? If you do you are mistaken. For true religion, like almighty God, the supreme author and object of it, is but one. Nor is there any essential difference between the religion of Jesus Christ and that of Adam in Paradise. And one reason why deists and free-thinkers contend for natural in opposition to revealed religion is because they do not understand it.' A little later, she sums up her position in this way: 'In a word, our Saviour came, not to teach us a new, but to retrieve the old, natural religion, and to put us again under the conduct of right reason, by the direction and assistance of His Holy Spirit.' To her it is self-evident, when one considers 'the present state of mankind', that 'the system of the Gospel is a most noble and reasonable institution'.[1]

It must be conceded that the spirit of 'reasonable religion', so beloved of the eighteenth century, has coloured Susanna's thought and language here. Yet we must be careful not to read too much into these passages. Susanna neither diluted the historic faith nor sought to empty it of its central mystery. In bringing together natural and revealed religion, she was not reducing the revelation in Christ to a few 'truths of reason' and a little dry morality. She was rather contending that natural religion, rightly understood, made just as searching demands on men as did revealed; but that with the revelation in Christ grace was made available to meet them. 'The rules of right reason are as severe as the precepts of the Gospel, being in truth all one . . . (and) . . . it would be impossible for man, in his present condition, to live according

[1] *W.H.S. Pubns.*, No. 3, p. 36f.

to those rules, had it not pleased God, by revelation, to put him in the way, and to promise him the assistance of His Holy Spirit that he may be able to do it.'[1]

It would be easy to assume that this strongly rational element in Susanna's piety was a deviation from the Puritanism in which she had been reared; easy, but misleading. The truth is, of course, that there was a distinct emphasis on the rational element in religion in the classical Puritan tradition itself. Richard Baxter was on occasion moved to tears in the pulpit, but he was no emotional ranter. His sermons, like those of John Wesley, made a carefully reasoned appeal to the hearer. In *The Reformed Pastor*, Baxter urges his fellow-ministers, 'We have reasonable creatures to deal with; and as they abuse their reason against truth, so they will accept better reason for it before they will obey. We must therefore see that our sermons be convincing, and that we make the light of Scripture and reason shine so bright in the faces of the ungodly, that it may even force them to see, unless they wilfully shut their eyes.'[2] The combination of Scripture and reason, so characteristic of Wesley too, is significant, and should make us wary of dismissing Puritan preaching as an anti-rational appeal to the emotions. In Baxter's view, sinners were to be converted, not by being swamped under a wave of feeling, but by being convinced of the overwhelming rationality and cogency of the Christian message: 'The great things which we have to commend to our hearers, have reason enough on their side, and lie plain before them in the Word of God; we should therefore be so furnished with all store of evidence, as to come as with a torrent upon their understandings, and bear down all before us, and with our dilemmas and expostulations to bring them to a nonplus, and pour out shame upon all their vain objections, that they may be forced to yield to the power

[1] *W.H.S. Pubns.*, No. 3, p. 36.
[2] Baxter, *Practical Works*, ed. Orme, XIV, 226.

of Truth and see that it is great, and will prevail.'[1] The appeal was to the mind and will, rather than to the emotions.

Dealing with ministerial teaching, on another occasion, Baxter asserts that a good minister will teach each of his people three basic truths: the knowledge of himself as 'A Rational free agent'; the knowledge of God as Creator and Ruler; and the knowledge that there is a life to come. He adds that the minister, in delivering these truths, 'needeth no supernatural proof of what he saith; but can prove it all to you from the light of nature.' These truths, however, only become savingly effective when they are known by 'supernatural grace' as well as by natural reason. 'These things . . . are (usually) at first apprehended by natural reason, not so as presently to put or prove the soul in a state of saving grace; but so as to awaken it to make further inquiry; and so when the soul is come so far as to see the same truths by supernatural Grace in the supernatural revelation of the Holy Scriptures, then they become more effectual and saving, which before were known but preparatorily: and so the same truths are then both the objects of knowledge and of faith.'[2] In assigning a high place to human reason, Baxter was not being disloyal to the Puritan tradition, though he is careful to qualify his exaltation of reason by stressing the need for revelation and saving grace.

Susanna's position is very similar. She thinks it self-evident that the existence of God is a truth apparent to any rational person: 'What creature under heaven, that has the use of reason, can be ignorant of the Being of God, and that they ought to live in subjection to him from whom they receive their own being?'[3] Yet such a knowledge is not saving knowledge, which can come only through 'a lively

[1] Ibid., loc. cit. See also Wm. Bates, *A Funeral-Sermon for . . . Mr Richard Baxter* (1692), p. 90.
[2] Baxter, *A Christian Directory*, Pt. III (1673), p. 719.
[3] Headingley MSS, A. f. 33.

151

faith in God's mercy through Christ'.[1] Here we are at the heart of Susanna's piety. Her theology and devotion are Christocentric, and have a personal warmth and ardour a world removed from the often cold or tepid faith of the Deist or Latitudinarian. Her devotion to the person of Christ comes out strongly in her exposition of the Creed, where under the head of 'The Life Everlasting' she asks, 'Who that has the lowest degree of faith would not part with all things in this world to obtain that love to our Blessed Redeemer, which we so long for, and sigh after?'[2] The same warmth of piety is evident in the way Susanna sometimes ends a meditation with a spontaneous ejaculation of praise, with a 'Glory be to thee, O Lord!' or a 'Glory be to the Father, Son, and Holy Ghost! Joint Authors of man's salvation!'[3]

Her emphasis upon reason is counterbalanced in three further ways. She sets careful bounds to the scope of reason; she maintains a profound sense of awe before the mystery of God's nature, will and purposes; and she stresses the illuminating and strengthening grace of the Holy Spirit. In all three respects her theology aligns her with, rather than detaching her from, the Puritan theological tradition. Susanna sets great store by reason, and yet for her its sovereignty is far from absolute. Its sway is that of a constitutional monarch hedged about by checks and balances, rather than a despot invested with Divine Right. Natural reason can convey to a man the truth that God is, and can shed a good deal of light on his duty to God and neighbour; but it can neither show him how human nature became corrupted nor how it has been redeemed. Introducing her exposition of the Creed (1710), Susanna argues that though 'that understanding and reason which is natural to all men', can know something of God's nature, 'yet, considering the present state of mankind,

[1] Headingley MSS, A. f. 50.
[2] Headingley MSS, C. f. 57.
[3] Headingley MSS, A. ff. 45, 58.

152

it was absolutely necessary that we should have some revelation from God to make known to us those truths upon the knowledge of which our salvation depends, and which unassisted reason could never have discovered', because man's 'understanding, will, and affections are extremely corrupted and depraved'.[1] Twenty-five years later, she writes in the same vein, in a letter to John: 'Would not some mention of the necessity of revealed religion be proper here? since, without it, all the wit of man could never have found out how human nature was corrupted at its fountain; neither had it been possible for us to have discovered any way or means whereby it might have been restored to its primitive purity.'[2]

Other saving truths which for Susanna are beyond the reach of unaided natural reason include: the Incarnation, the Atonement, the immortality of the soul, the Last Judgement, the Trinity, and the mystery of divine providence. Expounding the Creed, she declares: 'The infinite condescension of the eternal Son of God in assuming our nature was mysterious and incomprehensible, surpassing the wit of men or angels to conceive how such a thing might be.'[3] On the Crucifixion, she reflects that, 'Though stupid man could insensibly look on this mysterious passion of his blessed Redeemer, yet nature could not so behold her dying Lord, but by strong commotions expressed her sympathy.'[4] In the preliminary groundwork of her credal statement, she explains to her daughter Sukey that we could not have had 'any certainty of a future state, of the being of spirits, of the immortality of the soul, or of a judgement to come'.[5] In arguing against Aristotle's teaching that the world is eternal, she concludes: 'This error seems grounded on a true notion of the eternal, infinite Goodness of God, which he truly

[1] Headingley MSS, C. ff. 13–14.
[2] Clarke, *Wesley Family*, II, 28.
[3] Headingley MSS, C. f. 32; and see also Clarke, *Wesley Family*, II, 29.
[4] Headingley MSS, C. f. 41.
[5] Headingley MSS, C. f. 14.

supposes must eternally be communicating good to something or other, and it was his want of the knowledge of
Revealed Religion that probably led him into it. For had he
ever heard of that great article of our Christian Faith concerning the Holy Trinity, he had then perceived the
Almighty Goodness eternally communicating Being and all
the fulness of the Godhead to the Divine Logos, his uncreated
Word.'[1] Finally, in one of her daily meditations, her brooding
on the mystery of God's providence leads her to an ack-
nowledgement akin to the concluding lines of Isaac Watts'
great hymn to the Holy Trinity:

> Where reason fails, with all her powers,
> There faith prevails, and love adores.

Susanna bids herself bow down before the fathomless
wisdom of God: 'If you are now more rationally persuaded
that God is infinitely wise, then learn by this knowledge, to
practise a more hearty and universal subjection to him,
more cheerfully submit to the order of his Providence.
Submit your reason so far to your faith, as not to doubt or
scruple those points of faith which are mysterious to us
through the weakness of our understanding, and adore the
mystery you cannot comprehend.'[2]

The counterpart of the limitation of human reason in the
matter of salvation, is seen in Susanna's consistent emphasis
on the need for the assisting and illuminating grace of the
Holy Spirit. She draws a clear distinction, for example,
between knowing that God exists and is omnipotent, and a
personal knowledge of Him as Saviour. To realize from
Nature that there is an Almighty Creator is only 'to know
God as a man, as a reasonable creature; but this is not that
knowledge that leadeth us to eternal life'. She develops the
contrast between abstract, theoretical knowledge of God, and
that which is personal and experimental:

[1] Headingley MSS, A. f. 23.
[2] Headingley MSS, A. f. 61.

the one we attain in a scientifical method, by a long train of arguments, for which the bulk of mankind want either capacity or leisure; the other, by frequent and fervent application to God in prayer. The one is an effect of human reason assisted by human learning, peculiar to a few of more noble and refined sense; God perceived, known to the understanding as the creator, preserver and governor of the universe. The other is reason acting by the influence and direction of the Holy Spirit; God known to the heart, the will and its affections, not merely as the author of our being, but as he is exhibited to us under the character of a healer, a repairer of the lapse and misery of human nature, a Saviour, him whom our soul loveth.

Later the same day, she returns to the theme, and in language which is reminiscent of Pascal's strictures on 'the God of the philosophers', meditates: 'To know God only as a philosopher; to have the most sublime and curious speculations concerning his essence, his attributes, his providence . . . will avail us nothing, unless at the same time we know him experimentally; unless the heart perceive and know him to be her supreme good, her only happiness; unless the soul feel and acknowledge that she can find no repose, no peace, no joy, but in loving and being beloved by him.'[1] The centrality of the Spirit's work, and the warmth and vitality of Susanna's piety, which this passage exemplifies, are entirely typical.

For Susanna, indeed, the Christian life from first to last is life in the power and grace of the Holy Spirit. 'The first operation of the Holy Spirit in conversion is light to discern his state; the medium of which light is usually something extraordinary, either of judgement or mercy,'—a glance at the doctrine of special providences, so dear to the Puritans. By this illuminating grace of the Spirit, a man glimpses his own sinfulness and God's goodness, and is filled with 'regret and shame'. She concludes her meditation: 'This may be called a state of illumination, a good preparation, or disposition, for repentance. It is repentance in embryo.'[2]

[1] Headingley MSS, B. ff. 6–8.
[2] *Wesley Banner* (1852), IV, 203.

Elsewhere, she speaks of the refining power of the Spirit as, 'purifying your mind, exalting your nature to the dignity of a Divine resemblance, teaching you to undervalue, nay, despise the perishing enjoyments of what a mistaken world calls good, as unnecessary, or rather a hindrance to your spiritual and eternal good, which you will then prize above all others.'[1]

These quotations are typical, and it would be tedious to multiply them; but it is important to ask what they signify. What lies behind Susanna's stress on the severe limitations of reason, her warnings against abstract theologizing and a merely speculative knowledge of God? Why does she insist that, 'in the present state of human nature, no man can qualify himself for heaven without the Holy Spirit, which is given by God incarnate?'[2] May we not seek the clue to an answer in the spiritual crisis through which she had passed as an adolescent, in which speculative reason had led her away from the historic Faith into a passing involvement with Unitarianism? In one of her meditations, she records the benefits which had marked her early life:

Born in a Christian country; early initiated and instructed in the first principles of the Christian religion; good example in parents, and in several of the family; good books and ingenious conversation; preserved from ill accidents, once from violent death; married to a religious, orthodox man; by him first drawn off from the Socinian heresy, and afterwards confirmed and strengthened by B.B.——[3]

Adam Clarke suggests that 'B.B.——' refers to Bishop Bull, who in 1685, when Susanna was a girl of fifteen, published an influential defence of the doctrine of the Trinity, in his *Defensio Fidei Nicaenae*, as a reply to opponents who had charged him with being a Socinian.[4] If the orthodox in-

---

[1] *Wesley Banner* (1852), IV, 202. See also, on this same theme of the Holy Spirit in the Christian life, Headingley MSS, A. ff. 28, 30f., 58.

[2] Clarke, *Wesley Family*, II, 28. See also ibid., II, 63f.

[3] Ibid., II, 88.

[4] George Bull (1634–1710) became Rector of Suddington, near Cirencester, in 1685, and Bishop of St David's in 1705.

fluence which Samuel Wesley brought to bear on Susanna antedates, as seems probable, their marriage in 1689, Bishop Bull's work would qualify chronologically for the identification which Clarke suggests.

Whatever influences led her to return to orthodoxy, however, Susanna's altered belief was not only a change of heart. It was also emphatically a change of mind, which involved her in hard thinking and the disciplined use of reason. Henceforth for her reason and religion would be as closely conjoined as they were to become for her son John. If reason was the junior partner of the two, it was certainly not a sleeping one. Yet we may fittingly conclude this survey of Susanna's theology and devotion by citing a few passages from her writings which show clearly that the strongly rational element in her piety never ousted her profound sense of awe at the mystery of the Godhead. She reflects on the mystery of redemption: 'Consider the infinite, boundless goodness of the ever-blessed Trinity; adore the stupendous mystery of divine love! That God the Father, Son, and Holy Ghost, should all concur in the work of man's redemption! What but pure goodness could move, or excite God, who is perfect essential blessedness; that cannot possibly receive any accession of perfection or happiness from his creatures? What, I say, but love, but goodness, but infinite, incomprehensible love and goodness, could move him to provide such a remedy for the fatal lapse of his sinful unworthy creatures?'[1] Again, in her exposition of the Creed, the final clause ('And the life everlasting'), leads her to a great climax of praise and adoration:

How shall we blush to behold that exceeding and eternal weight of glory, that is conferred upon us for that little, or rather nothing, which we have done or suffered for our Lord! That God who gave us being, that preserved us, that fed and clothed us in our passage through the world; and, what is infinitely more, that gave his only Son to die for us; and has by his grace purified and

[1] *Wesley Banner* (1852), IV, 405-6.

conducted us safe to his glory. Oh, blessed grace! mysterious love! how shall we then adore and praise what we cannot here apprehend aright! How will love and joy work in the soul! But I cannot express it, I cannot conceive it. . . .[1]

Such reticent wonder was of the essence of the Puritan's 'serious godliness'.

[1] Clarke, *Wesley Family*, II, 71.

CHAPTER SIX

Defender of the Faith

> In the mean time I cannot but observe how signally
> God hath honoured those two Brethren (the *Wesleys*)
> by calling them forth, and enabling them, with great
> Power, to preach the Truth of the Gospel as it is in
> Jesus, and by setting His Seal to their Ministry. And
> am persuaded you will join with me in Prayer to our
> Lord, that He would strengthen and bless them more
> and more, and protect them from evil Men and evil
> Angels; and that they may be stedfast, immoveable,
> always abounding in the Work of the Lord, forasmuch
> as they know that their Labour is not in vain in the
> Lord. *Susanna Wesley*

THE last five years of Susanna's life, 1738–1742,
coincided with the beginnings of the Methodist Revival, and
all the turbulent controversy which its advent provoked. The
Revival came as a personal crisis for Susanna, not least
because her sons were divided in their attitudes towards it,
and appealed to the arbitrament of her religious insight and
sound common sense. Its emphasis upon religious experience, moreover, probed her personal convictions to their
depths, and offered her a chance of entering more fully than
ever before into the riches of her ancestral Puritanism.

Susanna, as will appear, was by no means uncritical of the Revival in its more extravagant tendencies. She was nearly seventy when it began, and viewed it through the wise and experienced eyes of 'an old disciple', as George Whitefield described her when he visited her during this period.[1] It says much for her, therefore, that though she was now an aged widow, who had found her husband's death in 1735 a hard blow to bear, she did not react towards the new movement with the natural and rooted conservatism of age. Once convinced that the new movement was inspired by the Spirit, she welcomed it positively and creatively, and indeed played a modest but decisive part in its course.

The first way in which the Revival impinged upon Susanna's life was by causing a rift within her family. Their religious experience of 1738 sharply divided John and Charles Wesley from their elder brother Samuel. Six letters written by Susanna have survived from the period 1738 to 1742, all of them concerned with the theology and experience of the Revival. Five were written to Charles, in reply to his passionate advocacy of the new teaching, and one to his brother Samuel, who had written his mother a fierce dissuasive from the Revival and all its works. Susanna's misgivings about some of the claims which John and Charles were making emerge clearly in this correspondence; but so does her basic acceptance of the Revival as the work of God's Spirit.

Susanna, chiefly through her son John, was rapidly brought into touch with the events which shaped the begininngs of the Methodist movement, from May 1738 onwards. John Wesley's classic description of the experience which was to prove a turning point in his life and work, sees it in terms of his personal realization of God's forgiveness and of the reality of justifying faith: 'I felt I did trust in Christ, Christ

[1] See *George Whitefield's Journals* (Banner of Truth Trust 1960), p. 212. Whitefield visited Susanna at Salisbury on the 13th February, 1739.

alone for salvation; and an assurance was given me that He had taken away *my* sins, even *mine*, and saved *me* from the law of sin and death.'[1] So he describes what happened to him at a quarter to nine on the evening of May 24th, 1738. A fortnight later he rode down to Salisbury to bid farewell to his mother before embarking on a journey to the Moravian settlement at Herrnhut in Germany. Significantly, he read to her on this occasion, 'a paper . . . containing a short account of what had passed in my own soul till within a few days of that time.' Wesley was no doubt gratified and enheartened at her reaction, for, 'She greatly approved it, and said she heartily blessed God, who had brought me to so just a way of thinking.'[2] Dr Martin Schmidt, in his fine and searching study of Wesley's theological development, plays down the importance of John's act in laying before his mother this chart of his spiritual odyssey. It is undeniable that he had for many years placed himself under her spiritual direction; but now, apparently, the leading-strings were severed. Wesley, in Dr Schmidt's judgement, 'no longer submitted theological questions to her. She only heard about his conversion from the Hutton family in an account which was distorted and tendentious, and it was for this reason that John read his own version of it to her. This pleased her, and she thanked God for her son's experience of salvation, yet it is remarkable that she did not recognize this document when it was sent to her by "a relation", accompanied by an unfavourable judgement about it. Furthermore, she agreed without reservation with this adverse opinion. Therefore the contents and the circumstances did not suggest to her that this was about John, and he himself was extremely surprised about this. This experience is sufficient to show how far she was now removed from him and his problems.'[3]

[1] Wesley, *Journal*, I, 476.
[2] Ibid., II, 219.
[3] M. Schmidt, *John Wesley, A Theological Biography*, I, 271f.

Wesley's own account of these events in his *Journal*, to which Dr Schmidt refers without quoting the vital passages, suggests that there has been a serious misreading of the evidence at several points. First, there is no trace of a suggestion in Wesley's account that he read this paper to his mother simply to set the record straight and disabuse her mind of the false impression she had received from a distorted version of the events. That came later. Secondly, the *Journal* makes plain that the 'relation', (probably Samuel Wesley, as Dr Schmidt, following Curnock, infers), did *not* send Susanna the actual paper she had heard John read, but his own highly-coloured paraphrase of it. Finally, John was *not* 'extremely surprised' that his mother did not recognize him in Samuel's account of the paper he had read to her. He merely reflected philosophically that it is hard to give an unbiased version of one's opponent's views, and admitted that he himself had not even recognized *his own account* in the distorted form in which Susanna had received it and reported it to him! Since this point is an important one, which bears closely on the whole relationship of mother and son, it will be well to quote the complete extract from the *Journal*, which Dr Schmidt unfortunately fails to do. Under the date Wednesday, 13th June 1739, Wesley records:

In the morning I came to London; and after receiving the Holy Communion at Islington, I had once more an opportunity of seeing my mother, whom I had not seen since my return from Germany.

I cannot but mention an odd circumstance here. I had read her a paper in June last year, containing a short account of what had passed in my own soul till within a few days of that time. She greatly approved it, and said she heartily blessed God, who had brought me to so just a way of thinking. While I was in Germany a copy of that paper was sent (without my knowledge) to one of my relations. He sent an account of it to my mother, whom I now found under strange fears concerning me, being convinced 'by an account taken from one of my own papers that I had greatly erred from the faith'. I could not conceive what paper that should be; but, on inquiry, found it was the same I had read her myself.—How hard is it to form a true judgement of any person or thing from the account of a prejudiced relator! Yea, though he be ever so honest a man—for he who gave this relation was one of unquestionable veracity. And yet by his *sincere* account of a writing which lay before his eyes was the truth so totally disguised that my mother knew not the paper she had heard from end to end, *not I that I had myself wrote.*[1]

If, then, John did not read this paper to his mother to counter the damage done by a biased account of his conversion, why did he read it? Here we must look closely at the nature of the document itself. In Dr Schmidt's narrative, we are told, 'She only heard about his conversion from the Hutton family in an account which was distorted and tendentious, and it was for this reason that John read his own version of it to her.' As we have seen, however, there is no ground for thinking that Susanna was left, initially, to learn of her son's experience by second-hand report. She had it direct from John himself two weeks after the event. What she apparently heard then, moreover, was not simply an account of what happened at Aldersgate Street on 24th May 1738, but something far more important and comprehensive. In John's own words, it was 'a short account of what had passed in my own soul till within a few days of that time'. John had had two weeks in which to reflect on the crisis of Aldersgate Street, to look back, and to read the whole story of his life in the light of it. The short account he read to his mother was a comprehensive attempt, in small compass, at what Richard Baxter's editor calls a 'Self-analysis and Life-review',[2] in true Puritan fashion. It was natural, surely, for John to read this account to his mother, for she had been the sovereign influence in his early spiritual development, and his constant mentor in his mature religious life.

One's first instinct is to sigh for a sight of this paper, which John presented, in some sense surely, for his mother's

[1] Wesley, *Journal*, II, 219–20. My italics in last seven words of quotation.
[2] See *The Autobiography of Richard Baxter*, ed. J. M. Lloyd Thomas, chapter X.

approval and confirmation. In it he would want above all
to knit up the ravelled skein of his spiritual development,
and integrate it into an ordered and coherent account. But
could any account be authentic which failed to commend
itself to the keen mind and spiritual perception of the mother
who had so largely shaped his spirit? What was the verdict
of the one who had been, through all the years, 'more
particularly careful of the soul of this child'? This occasion,
which Dr Schmidt dismisses rather brusquely as part of an
episode which merely underlines the gulf between mother
and son, is on the contrary profoundly significant of the
depth of their relationship. The whole sequence of events
cries out for attention, but has seldom been given it.[1] If only
we could lay our hands on Wesley's paper!

It would seem, however, that we have this very document
—or something remarkably like it—preserved for us by
Wesley himself. It is perhaps not generally realized that the
best-known passage in the *Journal*, the Aldersgate Street
narrative, is not an isolated account, though frequently
quoted as though it were. It is in fact paragraph 16 of an
eighteen-point statement, in which Wesley summarily
describes the course of his spiritual development during the
thirty-five years of his life. He prefaces this long entry for the
24th May, 1738, with the words: 'What occurred on *Wednesday* the 24th, I think best to relate at large, after premising
what may make it the better understood. Let him that cannot

---

[1] Dr J. E. Rattenbury's *The Conversion of the Wesleys* (1938), makes no reference to John's reading to his mother this account of his spiritual life up to and
including 24th May 1738; nor does Mrs Elsie Harrison in her *Son to Susanna*,
(1937), the theme of which is the decisive part Susanna played in her son's
development. Two works which do place the incident in the context of
Susanna's formative influence on John are, S. G. Dimond, *The Psychology of the
Methodist Revival* (1926), p. 56, and M. R. Brailsford, *A Tale of Two Brothers*
(1954), p. 121. Both, however, limit the scope of John's paper, Dr Dimond by
describing it as merely, 'a full account of his evangelical conversion', and Miss
Brailsford by calling it, 'a brief account of the religious experiences through
which he had been passing since his return to England.' Wesley's own description, however, gives no warrant for such temporal limitation of the period with
which the paper deals.

receive it ask of the Father of lights that He would give more
light to him and me.' His words imply a certain diffidence in
presenting this personal document to the reader. A similar,
though heightened, diffidence may be inferred from his
action in giving an account of himself to his mother. The
contents of this excursus in the *Journal* certainly tally with the
description he gave of the 'paper' he read to his mother,
namely, 'a short account of what had passed in my own soul
till within a few days of that time' (i.e. 8th June 1738).

The first paragraph of Wesley's account is of peculiar
interest for an understanding of Susanna's part in his
religious training and development. It deals with his early
years, until he was about ten and before he was sent away
to school. During these years at Epworth, his mother's influence was paramount. Her character, teaching, and devotion
helped to shape his soul, and the little private boarding
school which she in effect created, provided the *milieu* for
her children's growth in the Christian life. Wesley describes
these years as follows:

1. I believe, till I was about ten years old I had not sinned away
that 'washing of the Holy Ghost' which was given me in baptism;
having been strictly educated and carefully taught that I could
only be saved 'by universal obedience, by keeping all the commandments of God'; in the meaning of which I was diligently
instructed. And those instructions, so far as they respected outward duties and sins, I gladly received and often thought of.
But all that was said to me of inward obedience or holiness I
neither understood nor remembered. So that I was indeed as
ignorant of the true meaning of the law as I was of the gospel of
Christ.[1]

It is essential to note carefully exactly what Wesley says
here. The strictness of the religious upbringing of the Wesley
children has already been demonstrated from Susanna's own
account. Again, the consistent stress in Susanna's theology
and devotion upon complete obedience to God's will and

[1] Wesley, *Journal*, I, 465.

commands, has already been amply demonstrated. The heart of the paragraph lies in Wesley's distinction between 'outward duties and sins', and 'inward obedience or holiness'. The teaching he received under the first head, he had readily accepted; but that which related to 'inward obedience or holiness' had made no deep or lasting impression on him. So at least it seemed as he looked back from the vantage-point of his present profound experience of the inward working of God's grace. It is essential to note that he does not say that teaching about 'inward obedience or holiness' was not given. His words are: 'But all that was said to me of inward obedience or holiness I neither understood nor remembered.'

It may be that we can detect here, behind Wesley's qualifying 'But', an implied criticism of the bias of his religious education at Susanna's hands. We must allow fully for the circumstances in which he writes,—a quarter of a century after the events, in the full flush of a vivid religious experience, and telescoping ten years of his life into a paragraph. It is notoriously difficult to give an objective account of one's childhood impressions, and Wesley's circumstances hardly made for objectivity. Nevertheless, Susanna's own later misgivings over the expression which John and Charles gave to their experience of 1738, provides added ground for raising the question: had she really stressed, in her teaching of the children, the centrality of personal faith in Christ and of the justifying grace of God? The question is significantly reinforced by paragraph 11 of Wesley's account of his spiritual progress up to May 1738. While at Oxford, he had come to see that obedience to God's law must include inward holiness of heart and mind, and he had made a fierce but unsuccessful effort to conform to the standard. Georgia had taught him that his true need was for a living faith, but he did not yet understand what that involved. His meeting with the Moravian, Peter Böhler, on his return to England in January 1738, opened his eyes—after a struggle. When

Böhler 'affirmed of true faith in Christ (which is but one) that it had those two fruits inseparably attending it, 'dominion over sin and constant peace from a sense of forgiveness', I was quite amazed, and looked upon it as a new gospel. If this was so, it was clear I had not faith. But I was not willing to be convinced of this. Therefore I disputed with all my might, and laboured to prove that faith might be where these were not: for all the scriptures relating to this I had been long since taught to construe away: *and to call all Presbyterians who spoke otherwise.*'[1] 'Long since,' says Wesley. As long ago as those first ten years at Epworth? we might rejoin.

The question has disturbing implications, which may be spelled out as follows: was the central Reformation doctrine of justification by the free grace of God one which had been relegated to that part of Wesley's parents' Nonconformist past which they preferred to forget? Wesley's own account contains a hint of a negative answer, when he goes on to say that, convinced by Böhler of the need for this kind of faith, he resolved to seek it, first, 'By absolutely renouncing all dependence, in whole or in part, upon *my own* works or righteousness; on which I had really grounded my hope of salvation, *though I knew it not*, from my youth up.'[2] 'Though I knew it not'—here at least is an indication that Susanna had never inculcated any doctrine of justification by works. Wesley's evidence is supported by various passages in her own writings. Two other possibilities remain open. Had the doctrine of justification by grace and the need for personal faith—both so central to the Puritan tradition—become overlaid or attenuated in Susanna's teaching? It seems unlikely in view of the evidence of her own writings. Alternatively, did the very system of rules which she operated speak louder to her children's hearts and minds than her explicit

[1] Wesley, *Journal*, I, 471. My italics.
[2] Ibid., I, 472. The first italics are Wesley's, the second mine.

teaching on divine love? Did they feel themselves under the
Law, even though they were taught that they were under
grace? Possibly; though of the centrality of grace in Susanna's
theology there can be no real doubt at all.

Susanna certainly knew the meaning of justification by
grace through faith. She knew it, of course, from the Articles
and Homilies of the Church of England, where it had
received classic expression. She knew it too from the tradition
of Puritan piety in which she was bred. Her favourite Puritan
author, Baxter, expounds the doctrine in typical fashion:
'The sinner hath already found himself to be a stranger and
enemy to God, under the guilt of sin and curse of his law,
and knows there is no coming to him in peace till his case be
altered; and, therefore, having before been convinced, also,
that only Christ is able and willing to do this, and having
heard his mercy in the Gospel freely offered, his next act is,
secondly, to accept of Christ for Saviour and Lord.' All the
personal warmth of Puritan piety is found in Baxter's
insistence that this accepting of Christ is one which engages
the affections: 'I call it an affectionate accepting, though
love seem another act quite distinct from faith, and if you
take faith for assent only, so it is; yet I take it as essential to
that faith which justifies. To accept Christ without love, is
not justifying faith. Nor doth love follow as a fruit, but immediately concur; nor concur as a mere concomitant, but
essential to a true accepting.'[1]

It was in this tradition of devotion and theology that
Susanna had been reared. Its traces may be found scattered
through her own meditations and expositions, where she
speaks, typically, of the need for 'a lively faith in God's mercy
through Christ', and of her longing for a greater 'love for
our dear Redeemer.'[2] It is true that in her exposition of the

---

[1] Baxter, *The Saints' Everlasting Rest*, in *Practical Works*, ed. Orme, XXII,
192–3. For Susanna's quotation of Baxter on faith, in a letter to John Wesley
of 1732, see Stevenson, *Memorials of the Wesley Family*, p. 15.

[2] See above, p. 151f and Chapter Five, passim.

Creed (1710), she gives a rather tepid and intellectual definition of faith: 'By faith in Christ is to be understood an assent to whatever is recorded of him in Holy Scripture.'[1] Yet in her letters she reveals a much fuller and richer understanding of faith as essentially personal trust in Christ. Writing to John in 1735, she urges 'the knowledge and faith of Jesus Christ' to be absolutely necessary for salvation, and continues: 'By *faith*, I do not mean an assent only to the truths of the gospel concerning him, but such an assent as influences our practice; as makes us heartily and thankfully accept him for our God and Saviour upon his own conditions. No faith below this can be saving.'[2] Finally, we may quote another letter written before Susanna was confronted with the crisis of the Revival. Writing in 1737, to Mrs Alice Peard of Tiverton, she extols God's 'redeeming love and free grace', and expounds the meaning of justification: 'I verily think one reason why Christians are so often subject to despond is, that they look more to themselves than to their Saviour; they would establish a righteousness of their own to rest on, without adverting enough to the sacrifice of Christ, by which alone we are justified before God. But I need not say more, considering to whom I am writing; only give me leave to add one more request, which is, that you would commit your soul, in trust, to Jesus Christ, as God incarnate, in a full belief that he is able and willing to save you. Do this constantly, and I am sure he will never suffer you to perish.'[3]

Against this kind of background, Susanna's acceptance and understanding of John's experience of 1738 are much more readily intelligible. Her approval of the paper he read to her on 8th June 1738, no doubt helped to fire him to preach on Justification by Faith in his University Sermon at Oxford three days later. In a memorable exposition of Ephesians 2:8,

---

[1] Clarke, *Wesley Family*, II, 47.
[2] Ibid., II, 27.
[3] Ibid., II, 106.

Wesley sounded the trumpet-call of the Revival in terms which, though more passionate and explicit than those used by Susanna, were thoroughly in line with her beliefs. As in her writings, faith is 'not barely a speculative, rational thing, a cold lifeless assent, a train of ideas in the head; but also a disposition of the heart'. There is the same centrality given to the atoning work of Christ: 'Christian faith is then, not only an assent to the whole gospel of Christ, but also a full reliance on the blood of Christ; a trust in the merits of his life, death, and resurrection; a recumbency upon him as our atonement and our life, *as given for us*, and *living in us*; and, in consequence hereof, a closing with him, and cleaving to him, as our 'wisdom, righteousness, sanctification, and redemption', or, in one word, our salvation'.[1] Had John's mother been present in the congregation that was scandalized at his discourse that day, she might well have been uncomfortable in hearing him maintain, with scant qualification, that the justified man does not commit sin; but she would hardly have quarrelled with his exposition of saving faith.

Susanna's misgivings were roused, not by the message of justifying faith, but by the claims made in the Revival movement that every Christian should be assured of his forgiveness, and be able to specify the precise moment when he was granted justifying faith. One may diagnose her misgivings as evidence of a lowering of spiritual temperature caused by the transition from Puritanism to the Age of Reason. Alternatively, one may prefer to see here Susanna's fundamental reverence, her reticence in speaking of the ways of God, and her refusal to generalize from the experience of one soul and assert that He must deal similarly with all. We see her grappling with what to her were the doctrinal extravagances of the Revival in three letters she wrote to Charles Wesley in the period 1738–40. Her courteous and measured protests were provoked by that strain of ex-

[1] Wesley, *Works*, V. 9.

tremism in Charles's character, which displayed itself not only in the splendid hyperbole of his hymns, but also in some unbalanced statements of the doctrines which he preached. In her first letter, written in reply to Charles and dated 19th October 1738, she rejoices in his new experience of the saving power of Christ: 'Blessed be God, who showed you the necessity you were in of a Saviour to deliver you from the power of sin and Satan (for Christ will be no Saviour to such as see not their need of one), and directed you by faith to lay hold of that stupendous mercy offered us by redeeming love.' She ends, emphatically, with a doxology: 'No, there is none but Christ, none but Christ, who is sufficient for these things. But, blessed be God, he is an all-sufficient Saviour! and blessed be his holy name, that thou hast found him a Saviour to thee, my son! O let us love him much, for we have much forgiven.'[1] Her final sentence, however, shows that she is puzzled by one aspect of Charles's letter: 'I would gladly know what your notion is of justifying faith, because you speak of it as a thing you have but lately received.'

Susanna was even less satisfied by her son's explanation of his position, and on 6th December 1738, writes with typical forthrightness:

I think you are fallen into an odd way of thinking. You say that till within a few months you had no spiritual life, nor any justifying faith.

Now this is as if a man should affirm he was not alive in his infancy, because, when an infant, he did not know he was alive. All, then, that I can gather from your letter is, that till a little while ago you were not so well satisfied of your being a Christian as you are now.

Having transposed Charles's no doubt highly dramatic account of his recent experience into these sober and muted tones, Susanna goes on to welcome most cordially the new

---

[1] Clarke, *Wesley Family*, II, 116, correcting the 1823 edition, which reads, 'for we have much *to be* forgiven.' (Italics mine.)

depth of Christian life into which he has clearly entered: 'I heartily rejoice that you have now attained to a strong and lively hope in God's mercy through Christ. Not that I can think that you were totally without saving faith before: but it is one thing to have faith, and another thing to be sensible we have it. Faith is the fruit of the Spirit, and the gift of God; but to feel or be inwardly sensible that we have true faith, requires a farther operation of God's Holy Spirit.' Her closing paragraph is an index of her spirituality and common sense. She brings Charles back from preoccupation with his religious feelings, or lack of them, to the over-arching sovereignty of God and the certainty of His promises: 'You say you have peace, but not joy in believing: Blessed be God for peace! May this peace rest with you! Joy will follow, perhaps not very closely; but it will follow faith and love. God's promises are sealed to us, but not dated: there-fore patiently attend his pleasure; he will give you joy in believing. Amen.'[1] 'God's promises are sealed to us, but not dated': there, in a word, is the true Puritan's resolute submission to the sovereign will of God.

In this last letter, Susanna assures Charles that they are at one in their understanding of justifying faith, which she defines as 'trusting in Jesus Christ, or the promises made in him'. The main point on which she differs from him is, in her own words, that 'I do not judge it necessary to know the exact time of our conversion'.[2] By March 1739, however, her doubts about the Revival had been renewed and intensified by a detailed and hostile account of it sent her by her eldest son, Samuel. Samuel was as inflexible a High Churchman as his father had been, and believed the preaching of John and Charles to be subversive both of sound doctrine and good order in the Church. In two letters he communicated his worst fears to his mother. Susanna had no hesitation in

---

[1] Clarke, *Wesley Family*, II, 116.
[2] Clarke, *Wesley Family*, II, 117.

agreeing with his condemnation of those who sought assurance of salvation by 'pretensions to dreams, visions, &c.', or
to 'new revelations'. Such claims were tantamount to rejection of the divinely-appointed means of assurance, namely,
the 'Holy Scriptures, wherein all may find the rules by which
we must live here and be judged hereafter, so plainly laid
down, "that he who runs may read"; and it is by these laws
we should examine ourselves, which is a way of God's
appointment, and therefore we may hope for his direction
and assistance in such examination'. There was sound
Puritan teaching behind this insistence on bringing the
vagaries of individual experience to the touchstone of Scripture, and her reference to 'rules' and 'laws' had more to do
with a concern for objectivity than with legalism. She then
expounds her own doctrine of assurance, which involves an
examination of one's heart and life in the light of 'the conditions of the gospel covenant'. It is a delusion to hope for
assurance on any other terms:

if, upon a serious review of our state, we find that in the tenor
of our lives we have or do now sincerely desire and endeavour
to perform the conditions of the gospel covenant required on
our parts, then we may discern that the Holy Spirit hath laid in
our minds a good foundation of a strong reasonable, and lively
hope of God's mercy through Christ.

This is the assurance we ought to aim at, which the apostle
calls 'the full assurance of hope', which he admonishes us to
'hold fast unto the end'.

This assurance of hope is not the same as the confident
assurance of faith, involving peace with God and a conscious
experience of forgiveness, which we find in the teaching of
the Wesleys and in Puritanism. Assurance, or 'a hope of
God's mercy through Christ', is *inferred* from one's own
sincerity of heart and life in seeking to obey God's commands. This process is only Part One of Wesley's doctrine,
which he denotes by the title 'the witness of our own spirit'.
Susanna does not envisage the direct 'witness of God's Spirit',

applied by His grace to the heart of the believer. Both are requisite in Wesley's understanding of the New Testament, and may occur without any visionary experiences. On the basis of the inaccurate account she had received of her sons' teachings, however, Susanna naturally concludes that 'the consequence of encouraging fanciful people in this new way of seeking assurance (as all do that hear them tell their silly stories without rebuke), I think, must be turning them out of God's way into one of their own devising'. She wrote this letter from Devon, but was about to remove to London, where she hoped 'to see Charles; and then I can fully speak my sentiments of their new notions, more than I can do by writing'.

Her doubts and suspicions about the work John and Charles were doing, were unexpectedly assuaged by her meeting with George Whitefield, who paid her a visit before she left Devon, and did much to set her mind at rest. Whitefield's visit was a short one, interposed during a tour of the South-West in which he was trying to raise money for the Orphan House in Georgia. Susanna describes their meeting, at which she questioned Whitefield closely about her sons' 'way of living', expressed her dislike of their itinerant preaching, and voiced her fears that they were intent on making innovations in the Church: 'You have heard, I suppose,' she wrote to Samuel,

that Mr Whitfield is taking a progress through these parts to make a collection for a house in Georgia for Orphans, and such of the natives' children as they will part with to learn our language and religion. He came hither to see me, and we talked about your brothers. I told him I did not like their way of living, wished them in some place of their own, wherein they might regularly preach, &c. He replied, I could not conceive the good they did in London; that the greatest part of our clergy were asleep, and that there never was a greater need of itinerant preachers than now. Upon which a gentleman that came with him said that my son Charles had converted him, and that my sons spent all their time in doing good. I then asked Mr Whitfield if my sons were not for making some innovations in the church; which I much feared. He assured me they were so far from it, that they endeavoured all they could to reconcile dissenters to our communion; that my son John had baptized five adult presbyterians in our own way on St Paul's day, and he believed would bring over many to our communion.

Susanna was impressed with Whitefield's sincerity, and somewhat reassured by his report of what John and Charles were doing. She would have liked, however, a longer talk with him, and seems to have found his enthusiasm a trifle naive: 'His stay was short, so I could not talk with him so much as I desired. He seems to be a very good man, and one who truly desires the salvation of mankind. God grant that the wisdom of the serpent may be joined to the innocence of the dove!'[1]

Before Susanna wrote the last three letters in this series, she had experienced a conscious sense of the pardon of her sins, while receiving Holy Communion, in August 1739.[2] No doubt this experience made her more receptive towards the theology of the Revival and the preaching of her sons. Other factors reinforced this personal influence. She was now living with John Wesley at the Foundery in Moorfields, the head-quarters of the Methodist work in London, and so was in constant touch with Methodist faith and practice at first hand. Her eldest son, Samuel, who had continually warned her of the dangers he thought patent in the movement to which John and Charles had set their hands, died on 6th November 1739. She felt the loss of 'Son Wesley', as she called him, very deeply, and confided in a letter to Charles dated 29th November 1739: 'Your brother was exceeding dear to me in this life, and perhaps I have erred in loving him too well. I once thought it impossible to bear his loss, but none know what they can bear till they are tried.'

[1] Clarke, *Wesley Family*, II, 110–11. For Whitefield's own account of this meeting, see *George Whitefield's Journals* (1960), p. 112.

[2] See below, p. 197f.

Physical illness had also taken its toll of her strength: 'I cannot write much, being weak. I have not been downstairs above ten weeks, though better than I was lately.'[1]

Her last two letters to Charles show that bereavement and illness had had a depressive effect on her. She seems a frail old lady now, much less sure of herself, even more dependent on her sons, and inclined to reproach herself for a lack of real faith. In her middle years, when physical strain had induced a bout of accidie, she could diagnose her condition with unerring insight. Now, an aged widow, with her children for the most part gone from her, she simply has not power to do it. Her letter, written from the Foundery on 27th December 1739, is pathetic in its tone:

Dear Charles,

You cannot more desire to see me than I do to see you. Your brother, whom I shall henceforth call Son Wesley, since my dear Sam is gone home, has just been with me and much revived my spirits. Indeed, I have often found that he never speaks in my hearing without my receiving some spiritual benefit. But his visits are seldom and short, for which I never blame him, because I know he is well employed, and, blessed be God, hath great success in his ministry.

She no longer has any qualms about the work John is doing. Her sole regret now is that she sees so little of him. In her next sentence, she confesses her extreme sense of dependence on her two sons: 'But, my dear Charles, still I want either him or you; for, indeed, in the most literal sense, I am become a little child and want continual succour.'

What of the consolations of her religion? These are real, but she feels, even so, that she has fallen from the spiritual heights to which she was once accustomed. Once solitude had helped her to grow in grace and in the knowledge of God. Now she needs the 'comfort and support' of 'religious conversation', and the companionship of like-minded friends. She can only regard this as a symptom of spiritual decline,

---

[1] Quoted by Eliza Clarke, *Susanna Wesley*, p. 200f.

a pointer to her lack of faith: 'Formerly I rejoiced in the absence of company, and found the less I had of creature comforts the more I had from God. But alas! I am fallen from that spiritual converse I once enjoyed. And why is it so? Because I want faith. God is an omnipresent unchangeable God, in whom is no variableness neither shadow of turning; the fault is in myself, and I attribute all mistakes in judgement and all errors in practice to want of faith in the blessed Jesus.' When she goes on to reproach herself for being 'poor and low in faith and love', we must surely take full account of the lowering effects of age and illness and bereavement. Her letter was interrupted by the coming of visitors, who helped to lift her depression and alter the tone of her letter: 'I have been prevented from finishing my letter. I complained I had none to converse with me on spiritual things, but for these several days I have had the conversation of many good Christians, who have refreshed in some measure my fainting spirits; and though they hindered my writing, yet it was a pleasing and I hope not an unprofitable interruption they gave me.' She finishes on a strong note, with more than a trace of her old fire, as she gives robust expression to her support for the work her sons are doing: 'I hope we shall shortly speak face to face; and I shall then, if God permit, impart my thoughts more fully. But then, alas! when you come, your brother leaves me. Yet that is the will of God, in whose blessed service you are engaged, who has hitherto blessed your labours, and preserved your persons. That he may continue so to prosper your work, and protect you both from evil, and give you strength and courage to preach the true gospel in opposition to the united prayers of evil men and evil angels, is the hearty prayer of, dear Charles, Your loving mother, Susanna Wesley.'[1]

The last personal letter which has survived from Susanna was written to Charles from the Foundery on 2nd October

[1] Printed in Eliza Clarke, *Susanna Wesley*, pp. 201–2.

1740.[1] Charles had evidently sent her a letter criticizing her theological position, and his words had served only to strengthen her self-condemnation and to deepen her spiritual depression. At the level of piety and personal devotion, Susanna accepts his strictures almost unreservedly: 'I thank you for your kind letter; I call it so, because I verily believe it was dictated by a sincere desire of my spiritual and eternal good. There is too much truth in many of your accusations: nor do I intend to say one word in my own defence, but rather choose to refer all things to Him that knoweth all things.' No doubt experience had taught her the wisdom of not getting involved in protracted theological controversy with her voluble son. On the other hand, we may question Charles's pastoral and filial sense of fitness in dealing with his mother in this heavy-handed and unfeeling way, when she was clearly at a low ebb spiritually. The effect of his criticisms in deepening her depression may be seen in her next paragraph: 'This I must tell you: you are somewhat mistaken in my case. Alas! it is far worse than you apprehend it to be! I am not one of those who have never been enlightened, or made partaker of the heavenly gift, or of the Holy Ghost, but have many years since been fully awakened, and am deeply sensible of sin, both original and actual.' Charles has apparently been dealing with her, characteristically, as one who has not yet really seen the light, whereas she herself is conscious of having seen it but sinned against it. She goes on: 'My case is rather like that of the Church of Ephesus; I have not been faithful to the talents committed to my trust, and have lost my first love.'

This letter makes clear that the spiritual depression in which she finds herself has been with her for some time. She is tempted to despair, but finds new hope in her experience of the previous year, when at the sacrament she had entered into a deeper realization of forgiveness. 'I do not, and by the

[1] Printed Eliza Clarke, *Susanna Wesley*, pp. 204–6.

grace of God I will not, despair; for ever since my sad defection, when I was almost without hope, when I had forgotten
God, yet I then found He had not forgotten me. Even then
He did by His Spirit apply the merits of the great Atonement
to my soul, by telling me that Christ died for me. Shall the
God of truth, the Almighty Saviour, tell me that I am interested in His blood and righteousness, and shall I not believe
Him? God forbid! I do, I will believe.' If we ask what was
the occasion of her 'sad defection', which left her 'almost
without hope', it seems likely that the answer lies in her
reaction to her husband's death in 1735. When Samuel's
death seemed only a matter of time, in March 1735, Charles
wrote to his brother Samuel, 'My mother seems more cast
down at the apprehension of his death than I thought she
could have been.'[1] In November of that year, after Samuel
had died in the April, Susanna confessed in a letter to John
that though she had now 'no taste, no relish left for anything
the world calls pleasure, yet I do not long to go home, as in
reason I ought to do'.[2] Such references suggest that her pro-
longed depression may well have been the result of her
bereavement.

Yet however much she may have deferred to her son
Charles on the level of personal piety, in her theology she still
showed something of her old sturdy independence and good
sense. Charles, with his volatile temperament, was apt to
take the variations in his spiritual fervour much too seriously.
He had apparently been saying that he was not a Christian
any longer. Susanna retorts: 'I cannot conceive why you
affirm yourself to be no Christian, which is in effect to tell
Christ to His face that you have nothing to thank Him for,
since you are not the better for anything He hath yet done or
suffered for you. Oh! what great dishonour, what wondrous
ingratitude, is this to the ever-blessed Jesus? I think myself

[1] See above, p. 95.
[2] Quoted in Eliza Clarke, *Susanna Wesley*, p. 185.

179

far from being so good a Christian as you, or as I ought to be; but God forbid that I should renounce the little Christianity I have; nay, let me rather grow in grace and in the knowledge of our Lord and Saviour Jesus Christ. Amen.' Her last word is a pungent if measured criticism of certain tendencies towards a rather extravagant subjectivism which she found in early Methodist piety. Much as she owed to the fellowship of the Methodists at the Foundery, her spiritual maturity would not allow her to think them faultless. Her rebuke to Charles becomes a general one, directed to this reprehensible tendency to look more at one's spiritual state than at God's gracious acts in Christ: 'I find this is a way of talking much used among this people, which has much offended me; and I have often wished they would talk less of themselves and more of God. I often hear loud complaints of sin, &c., but rarely, very rarely, any word of praise and thanksgiving to our dear Lord.'[1] That was a warning note that clearly needed sounding. It says much for Susanna that she was able to rise above her own state of spiritual weakness and to sound it.

Constructive criticism of the tendency of some Methodists to be obsessed with their own religious experience, was not the only service Susanna rendered to the new movement. At this same period, her independence of judgement was exercised in a practical way, which was to be decisive for the whole future of Methodism. Her advice to John Wesley in a crisis has earned her the title of patroness of Methodist lay preachers. Thirty years before, when she had held devotional meetings in the rectory at Epworth, she had read a sermon as well as taking prayers, so that John could write of her that 'even she (as well as her father and grandfather, her husband, and her three sons) had been, in her measure and degree, a preacher of righteousness'.[2] It was her timely

[1] See also Richard Baxter, whom Susanna so admired, on this same theme, in Baxter, *Autobiography*, ed. J. M. Lloyd Thomas, p. 113.
[2] Wesley, *Journal*, III, 32.

remonstrance that checked Wesley's hasty reaction to the unauthorized preaching of his young lay helper, Thomas Maxfield. John had hurried back to the Foundery from Bristol on hearing of this innovation, and his displeasure is patent in his curt words to his mother on arrival: 'Thomas Maxfield has turned preacher, I find.' Here, as so often before, John was to heed his mother's calm warning: 'John, you know what my sentiments have been. You cannot suspect me of favouring readily anything of this kind. But take care what you do with respect to that young man, for he is as surely called of God to preach as you are. Examine what have been the fruits of his preaching, and hear him also yourself.'[1] The words are typical of Susanna, both in their sweet reasonableness and in their bold, prophetic note. John acted on them, heard Maxfield preach, and was persuaded 'It is the Lord!' In so doing he gave his blessing to the order of Methodist lay preachers. Incidentally, the whole episode serves to refute Dr Schmidt's suggestion that after 1738 Susanna grew remote from an understanding of her son's problems, and had little or no influence on his work. In fact, the evidence suggests that the old relationship held, and that she maintained an informed and critical interest in all the varied aspects of the Revival, whose course she watched from the Foundery headquarters where she had made her home.

One final piece of evidence may be cited to show that Susanna, though critical of the Revival in some of its aspects, was yet basically committed to it in sympathy and support. The document in question is a twenty-eight-page pamphlet published as a contribution to the debate on Predestination

[1] H. Moore, *The Life of the Rev. John Wesley A.M.*, 2 vols. 1824–5, I. 506 Adam Clarke's description of the incident leaves little doubt that the account derives from Wesley himself. Clarke records, 'She said (I have had the account from Mr Wesley himself), "My son, I charge you before God, beware what you do; for Thomas Maxfield is as much called to preach the gospel as ever you were!"' (*Wesley Family*, II, 123.) Oral tradition seems to have heightened the imperative tone of Susanna's words, but the sense is substantially the same.

which broke out into print after Wesley's sermon on 'Free Grace' in 1740. The publication of this sermon provoked a Calvinist reply from George Whitefield, entitled *A Letter to the Reverend Mr John Wesley : In Answer to his Sermon, entituled, Free-Grace* (1741). This *Letter* in turn drew a spirited defence of Wesley in the form of the sixpenny pamphlet referred to, with the title, *Some Remarks on a Letter from the Reverend Mr Whitefield to the Reverend Mr Wesley, in a Letter from a Gentlewoman to her Friend*. This defence was anonymous, but all the evidence, both internal and external, points conclusively to Susanna as the writer of it. Richard Viney, one of Wesley's helpers at Newcastle, came across this pamphlet in cataloguing the library at the Orphan House, and recorded in his diary for 27th May 1744, 'Mr W. told me his Mother wrote it.'[1] Style and content, moreover, both point to Susanna's authorship.[2] She deals very sternly with Whitefield, whose 'Youth and Inexperience renders him somewhat pitiable',[3] and dismisses his professions of respect for Wesley as mere hypocrisy: 'As to his Compellations to Mr *Wesley* of Honoured and Dear, &c. I look upon them only as so many cant Words which are of no Signification, tho' possibly he might intend, by the frequent Use of them, to cut his Friend's Throat with a Feather.'[4]

Susanna goes on to deal with Whitefield's doctrine, and gives short shrift to Calvinism. She not only defends Wesley's claim that if predestination is true, 'then is all Preaching vain', but goes further: 'Mr *Wesley* speaks too modestly here,

[1] The evidence for Susanna's authorship is set out in an article by Dr Frank Baker in *Proceedings of the W.H.S.*, Vol. XXXV, 68–71, 'Susanna Wesley, Apologist for Methodism.'

[2] Compare, for example, the paragraph from the anonymous pamphlet which stands at the head of this chapter (see above, p. 159), with the section of Susanna's letter (27th December 1739) to Charles Wesley, quoted on p. 177 above. Both extracts commend the work of the Wesley brothers to God's blessing and protection, against the opposition of 'evil men and evil angels'.

[3] See above p. 175 for Susanna's implied criticism of Whitefield's naivety at their meeting in 1739.

[4] *Letter from a Gentlewoman to her Friend* (1741), p. 3.

in only saying Preaching is vain . . . he might have safely affirmed preaching the Gospel to be a cruel Ordinance: For if, as *Calvin* says, *God speaketh by his Ministers to Reprobates that they may be deafer; he gives Light to them that they may be the blinder* . . . what good Man would not rather choose to be a Hangman than a Minister of the Gospel?'[1] The bulk of the tract has nothing to do with personalities, but is a powerful theological refutation of Calvinism, in which Susanna sets forth Christ as the Second Adam, embodying God's redemptive purpose, not for some predetermined number of the elect, but for the whole human race. She also defends the Wesleys' teaching on Christian Perfection, as being couched in terms of 'Gospel Holiness' and not 'absolute Perfection'. The pamphlet shows Susanna as a formidable theologian, a convinced Methodist, and (against her will) a skilled and hard-hitting controversialist. Her reluctance in writing this piece is clear from the distaste for controversy she expresses, and which her life and character both bear out. Her father would no doubt have endorsed her view that, 'Young Men, and Novices in Divinity, commonly delight in Controversy; but sober, experienced Christians, much abhor it; well knowing, that it usually destroys the Vitals of true saving Religion; and that while men are disputing the Way, the Power of Godliness is lost.'[2] That she overcame this reluctance and entered the lists is surely testimony that this sober, experienced Christian was by now passionately convinced that she had found the power of godliness among the people called Methodists.

[1] *Letter from a Gentlewoman to her Friend*, p. 7.
[2] Ibid., p. 10.

CHAPTER SEVEN

Methodist Matriarch

The true founder of the Methodists was Mrs Wesley.
Julia Wedgwood
The Wesleys' mother was the mother of Methodism in
a religious and moral sense. *Isaac Taylor*

IT is no mere genealogical figure of speech to
describe Susanna as the mother of Methodism, as if simply
to underline the obvious fact that John and Charles Wesley,
as her sons, were greatly indebted to her in respect of both
character and training. If that were all, it would be more
accurate, though pedantic, to speak of her as the grandmother of Methodism. Yet *mother* is correct, for in a real
sense it was she who founded Methodism in Epworth
rectory, where we may see in germ the Methodist pattern of
discipline and pastoral oversight, with their careful framework of rules for Christian living. Susanna sponsored
Methodism not only *through* her sons, but also *in* them.

It is significant that more than a little of the doctrine,
ethos and polity of the early Methodist societies was fore-
shadowed in Mrs Wesley's household. She was herself the

embodiment of the 'serious godliness' which had characterized the Puritans, and which Methodism was in turn to
breed in its people. Several of the leading emphases of
Methodist theology may be discerned in her devotion and its
richly varied background. Dr Martin Schmidt, in his notable
'theological biography' of John Wesley, gives an impressive
synopsis of the Christian heritage into which he was born,
and describes the home at Epworth as one in which there
were brought together,

the heritage of Puritanism, Anglican churchmanship, and that
concern for the care of souls, social activity and missionary zeal,
derived from the revival of the Religious Societies. At the same
time it drew its sustenance from Puritan culture of family life and
from the nurture of individual souls found in Romanic mysticism.
To this was joined the influence of the Halle type of pietism.
Finally a place was given to liberal scholarship, and the har-
monious, mystical piety of a Henry Scougal was held in high
esteem. To all this was added Susanna Wesley's personal gift as a
teacher. Although this was charismatic in the deepest sense of
the word, it was nevertheless most methodically cultivated and
practised. Through this rich polyphony one leading theme
resounds like a *cantus firmus*: it is that of the love of God which
empowers man towards perfection. It might almost be said that
here, in the cradle, the main content of John Wesley's thought
was already being proclaimed.[1]

Dr Schmidt's passage brings out several points which have
already emerged in this present study: the central importance
of Susanna in the transmission of this theological heritage;
the profound influence of the Puritan tradition, stemming
from Dr Annesley, personified in Susanna, and formatively
at work in John Wesley; and the dominant theological motif
of 'the love of God which empowers man towards perfection'.
All these points need to be amplified, and might well serve as
text for this chapter.

If we attempt to trace Susanna's influence on the later
doctrinal formulations of Methodism, we may appropriately

[1] M. Schmidt, *John Wesley, A Theological Biography*, I, 63.

begin with an examination of the 'grand depositum',[1] the doctrine which Wesley regarded as Methodism's peculiar trust, that of Christian Perfection. Describing the manifold sources of Wesley's teaching, John L. Peters writes: 'Wesley brought the contributions not only of Taylor, Law and à Kempis, but also of Clement of Alexandria, Plotinus, Augustine, Tauler, the Cambridge Platonists, Molinos, Antoinette Bourignon, Madame Guyon, Macarius the Egyptian, François de Sales, Juan de Castaniza, Fénelon, and Pascal. From among these writers representing as they do the mystical tradition of the Church, it is obvious that Wesley was most influenced by the practical type.'[2] Dr Colin Williams, in his lucid study *John Wesley's Theology Today*, endorses this analysis, calls attention to the further influence of the Apostolic Fathers on Wesley's teaching, and underlines J. S. Simon's insight into the importance of the quest for holiness in the Religious Societies of eighteenth-century England.[3] Dr Williams makes, however, no reference to the importance of the theme of Christian Perfection in the Puritan tradition to which Wesley stood heir.[4] Yet we can trace this *motif*, in the writings of Susanna's father, in the Puritan divines whom she herself read, in her own meditations and treatises, and in the impressive series of Puritan classics which Wesley edited for his *Christian Library*.

The theme of Christian Perfection, as understood in the Puritan tradition, requires a rather fuller quotation from the significant passage in one of Dr Annesley's sermons which defines 'serious Christianity' as comprising essentially 'Christ and Holiness'. The sermon inevitably challenges comparison with Wesley's own understanding of Christian Perfection in

---

[1] Wesley, *Letters*, VIII, 238.
[2] J. L. Peters, *Christian Perfection and American Methodism* (1956), p. 20.
[3] C. W. Williams, *John Wesley's Theology Today* (1960), p. 173.
[4] The index of *John Wesley's Theology Today*, though the work treats its subject in historical depth as well as in contemporary significance, contains not a single reference to the Puritans.

terms of 'sanctification by faith', for it firmly eschews all idea of merit and sees Christian goodness as issuing fundamentally from faith in Christ. Annesley urged his congregation to

Remember these two words, though you forget all the rest of the Sermon, viz., 'CHRIST and Holiness, Holiness and CHRIST:' interweave these all manner of ways, in your whole conversation . . . Press after holiness as much as is possible, had you no CHRIST to befriend you; (for it is a shame to mind holiness the less, for any benefits you expect from CHRIST;) and rest as entirely upon CHRIST, as if there were nothing else required: (for the best of your holiness doth not merit acceptance).[1]

He went on to sum up the meaning of Christianity as essentially 'faith working by love', and to call for 'a holy faith, full of good works', quite in John Wesley's style.

Dr Annesley's sermon subjects are often illuminating in their bearing on this theme of Christian Perfection. He preached on Acts 24:16, 'And herein do I exercise myself, to have always a conscience void of offence toward God, and toward men', in an attempt to resolve the question, 'How may we be universally and exactly conscientious?'[2] On another occasion, he expounded Matthew 22:37–8, and addressed himself to another practical 'case of conscience': 'How may we attain to love God with all our hearts, souls, and minds?' He described the Christian's heart as completely on fire with the love of God: 'When the love of God is shed abroad in the heart, 'tis as the breaking of a Ball of lightning, it sets all on a flame immediately. It is the unspeakable enlargement of the heart towards God; the highest Rhetorick is too flat to express it, as is obvious in that Song of Songs, that Song of loves.'[3] In sermons such as these, we are close to Wesley's understanding of entire sanctification as a life transformed by an all-pervading love to God and man.

In his sermon on loving God with all one's powers, Dr

[1] *Christian Library*, ed. Wesley, XXIV, 453ff.; and see above, p. 40.
[2] *The Morning-Exercise at Cripplegate*, ed. Annesley, p. 1.
[3] *A Supplement to the Morning-Exercise at Cripplegate*, ed. Annesley, p. 3.

Annesley expounded in detail 'What it is to love God with the whole heart,' and stressed that 'perfect Hatred and perfect Love knows no such thing as the world calls Prudence'. He continued by defining carefully what this total love to God involved: 'Some expound this totality by this distinction: we are to love God with the whole heart positively and negatively: positively, where all powers of the will are set to love God, and this we cannot perfectly do while we are travellers, till we come to our heavenly country; but negatively, thou shalt so love God, that nothing contrary to the love of God shall be entertained in thy heart; and this we may attain to a pretty tolerable perfection of in this life.'[1] 'A pretty tolerable perfection in this life' is hardly the language of exact theological definition, but it does suggest a real affinity with Wesley's teaching. The likeness of this whole exposition to Wesley's doctrine is quite striking: perfection is interpreted essentially in terms of love to God; it is a modified perfection, suitable to the Christian in his earthly pilgrimage and not fully anticipating the life of heaven; and it consists in a sincerity of heart which does not entertain any impulse contrary to the love of God.

Annesley gave both warning and encouragement to his hearers, by urging that the supreme commandment of entire love to God, 'includes the highest perfection possibly attainable in this life; yet let not this difficulty fright you, for through Christ our sincere love (though weak) is accepted; and our imperfect love (because growing) shall not be despised.'[2] It is instructive to compare these extracts from a Puritan sermon of his grandfather with Wesley's own definitive expression of his teaching in *A Plain Account of Christian Perfection*, where he catechizes himself in the following terms:

Question. What is Christian Perfection?
Answer. The loving God with all our heart, mind, soul, and

---

[1] *A Supplement to the Morning-Exercise at Cripplegate*, ed. Annesley, p. 5.
[2] Ibid., p. 11.

strength. This implies, that no wrong temper, none contrary to love, remains in the soul; and that all the thoughts, words, and actions, are governed by pure love.[1]

Both Annesley and Wesley are agreed that man's love to God is itself a gift of the Spirit. Annesley points out that 'Our love to God is nothing else but the echo of God's love to us', and after appealing to Aquinas and De Sales, concludes: ' 'Tis the Lord alone that can direct our hearts into the love of God.'[2] Like Wesley, Annesley is careful to qualify the 'perfect love' to which the Christian is called, by a recognition that it can and does co-exist with certain 'unavoidable infirmities'. To one who doubts whether he truly loves God, the Puritan pastor counsels, 'Keep a severe watch against all sins; yet give not way to drooping fears, because of unavoidable infirmities,' and quotes Psalm 130:3–4, 'If thou, Lord, shouldest mark iniquities, O Lord, who shall stand?'

Dr Annesley's earnest emphasis upon Christian Perfection was not lost upon his children. According to Timothy Rogers, part of the dying prayer of Susanna's sister, Elizabeth, was that God would not only pardon her sins, but 'perfect holiness' in her.[3] Susanna herself, in a letter to John Wesley written in 1725, addressed herself to this same theme, in phrasing which is reminiscent of Wesley's developed teaching: 'And when, by the grace of God's Holy Spirit, we are so far conquerors, as that we never willingly offend, but still press after greater degrees of Christian perfection, sincerely endeavouring to plant each virtue in our minds, that may through Christ render us pleasing to God; we shall then experience the truth of Solomon's assertion, "The ways of virtue are ways of pleasantness, and all her paths are peace." '[4] Susanna's language may lack some of the warmth of her father's and son's formulations of the call to perfection,

---

[1] Wesley, *A Plain Account of Christian Perfection* (*Works*, XI, 394).
[2] *A Supplement to the Morning-Exercise at Cripplegate*, ed. Annesley, p. 12.
[3] T. Rogers, *Character of a Good Woman*, p. 159.
[4] Clarke, *Wesley Family*, II, 18.

but there is no mistaking the same earnestness and zeal. She does not speak of the heart aflame with love to God, as they do; and her call to 'plant each virtue in our minds' sounds a trifle studied and intellectual as a description of the *pugna spiritualis* of the would-be saint. Nevertheless, the doctrinal affiliations with John's later teaching are notable. They include: a stress upon the 'grace of God's Holy Spirit;' the safeguard against any doctrine of merit contained in the statement that it is only 'through Christ' that our virtues can 'render us pleasing to God'; the description of Christians as 'conquerors' of sin; the content of this state of Christian maturity as one in which we 'never willingly offend'; and the open-ended nature of 'perfection' in this life, in which we 'still press after greater degrees of Christian perfection'.

We may also trace a certain continuity between the Puritan tradition as expressed in Susanna's life and character, and later Methodist teaching, in the area of doctrine denoted by 'Assurance' or the witness of the Holy Spirit. According to this doctrine, based largely on Romans, Chapter 8, the believer may be assured that he enjoys peace with God and that his sins are forgiven. There is a brief reference to Puritan teaching on this head in Dr Arthur Yates' *The Doctrine of Assurance*,[1] though the book refers specifically only to the Westminster Assembly's Confession of Faith and the writings of John Owen. A much more systematic and complete exposition of Puritan thought on the witness of the Spirit is given by Dr G. F. Nuttall in his *The Holy Spirit in Puritan Faith and Experience* (1946). For our present purpose it will be helpful to supplement these writings by drawing on the works of the Puritan divines of Dr Annesley's circle, and by examining Annesley's own teaching and experience.

One of Annesley's co-preachers at the Morning Exercise,

[1] A. S. Yates, *The Doctrine of Assurance, with special reference to John Wesley* (1952), p. 172.

Thomas Doolittle, gave a detailed treatment of Assurance in his sermon on 1 John 5:13, 'These things have I written unto you that believe on the name of the Son of God; that ye may know that ye have eternal life.' He put the 'case of conscience' he had set himself to resolve in the form of the query, 'If we must aim at Assurance, what should they do, that are not able to discern their own spiritual condition?' He first set out his major proposition, 'That a believer without extraordinary revelation, might certainly know that he hath justifying faith, and unfeigned love to Christ, and that he is upright and sincere with God.'[1] Such knowledge derived basically from the Christian's awareness of the presence of the Spirit in his heart and life: 'A believer may know that he shall be saved, because he may know that he hath the Spirit of God dwelling in him. The in-dwelling of the Spirit is proper and peculiar to believers; for the world cannot receive him . . . That they have the Spirit, they may know by the special effects which he produceth in that heart where he dwells; by his convincing, humbling, sanctifying work . . . by his special assistance vouchsafed to them in holy prayer . . . by enabling them to mortify their sins more and more.' To help bring peace to troubled consciences, Doolittle gave a detailed series of 'Directions to get assurance', of which the first was to have recourse to Scripture: 'Get some characteristical distinguishing signs of true saving grace, by thy serious searching the word of God.' He then counselled self-examination, and a testing of one's state of soul by the touchstone of Scripture: 'Set thy conscience on work, and reflect upon thy own heart, and upon the motions of thy will, and compare thy self with the word of God.' The next direction was a call to prayer, to 'pray importunately for the witness of the Spirit of God'. He then entered a caveat which Wesley endorsed in his sermons on the witness of the Spirit, namely that

---

[1] *The Morning-Exercise at Cripplegate*, ed. Annesley, p. 308.

The Spirit never witnesseth any thing to any man contrary to
what is revealed in the Word, for he is a Spirit of Truth, and
never speaks contradictions; therefore if any man thinketh that
he hath the witness of the Spirit, testifying that he is a child of
God, and yet is not holy, humble, penitent, he is deceived; but
if thou hast the graces of the Spirit, and the Spirit witnesseth so
much unto thy conscience,

then all is well. The remaining directions were concerned to
stimulate growth in grace ('Press after the highest degrees
of grace . . .'), and to stress the vital importance of Christian
fellowship in this whole process ('Prize the society of the
people of God, that are acquainted with the workings of
God's Spirit upon their hearts . . .').[1]

This appeal to experience in religion was of course common to both Puritanism and Methodism; but lest 'experience' should seem to put a premium on the emotional
delights of religion, Doolittle added a final word of
warning:

Always be more observant of the purpose and disposition of thy
heart, the inclination of thy will, the general scope of thy life,
than the passionate sense of joy and comfort . . .
There is but little constancy in these joys, like the tide, they
ebb and flow. . . . Joys are the sweetmeats of the soul, but are
not for its constant fare and diet; for a spiritual banquet, not for
a standing-dish.[2]

Similarly Richard Baxter deprecates the interpretation of
the Spirit's witness in terms of mere personal feelings. Indeed
this grossly subjective approach had for a long time prevented
his realizing the vital necessity of the doctrine. In a very
interesting section of his autobiography he sets out the
cardinal importance for faith and practice of the witness of
the Spirit in the life of the believer:

I am now, therefore, much more apprehensive than heretofore
of the necessity of well grounding men in their religion, and
especially of the witness of the indwelling Spirit; for I more

[1] *The Morning-Exercise at Cripplegate*, ed. Annesley, pp. 313, 318–19.
[2] *The Morning-Exercise at Cripplegate*, ed. Annesley, p. 321.

sensibly perceive that the Spirit is the great witness of Christ and
Christianity to the world. And though the folly of fanatics
tempted me long to overlook the strength of this testimony of the
Spirit, while they placed it in a certain internal assertion or
enthusiastic inspiration, yet now I see that the Holy Ghost in
another manner is the witness of Christ and his agent in the
world. The Spirit in the prophets was his first witness; and the
Spirit by miracles was the second; and the Spirit by renovation,
sanctification, illumination and consolation, assimilating the soul
to Christ and heaven, is the continued witness to all true believers.
And if any man have not the Spirit of Christ, the same is none
of his.[1]

It is clear from these extracts that the Puritan preachers of
Dr Annesley's circle did not mean by assurance the private
inner feelings of the individual. That would have been to
leave the door wide open to enthusiasm (in the pejorative
sense), hypocrisy, and Antinomianism. These writers make
plain that there are objective criteria which the Christian
must use to test his own estimate of his spiritual condition:
the guiding light of Scripture, the counsel and advice of
fellow-Christians, and the moral content of his life and
character, which, if he were sincere, would bear the marks of
Christ's grace and goodness.

This same distinction between true and false assurance
was brought out by Daniel Williams, another friend of
Annesley, in a controversial work written against the views
of Dr Tobias Crisp, *Gospel Truth Stated and Vindicated*.
Williams denounced Crisp's view that 'Assurance is not
attained by the evidence of Scripture-marks or signs of grace,
or by the Spirit's discovering to us that he hath wrought in
our hearts any holy qualifications; but assurance comes only
by an inward voice of the Spirit, saying, Thy sins are for
given thee, and our believing thereupon that our sins are

---

[1] Baxter, *Autobiography*, ed. Lloyd Thomas, p. 110. See also Thomas Brookes,
Heaven on Earth, a Treatise on Christian Assurance (1654), reprinted 1961 by The
Banner of Truth Trust; and Baxter, *The Saints' Everlasting Rest* (*Practical Works*,
ed. Orme XXII, 491ff).

forgiven'.[1] In opposition to such teaching, which clearly put a premium on self-delusion, Williams expounded the classic Puritan doctrine of assurance, in terms which Wesley would readily have accepted:

The ordinary way whereby a man attaineth a well-grounded assurance, is not by immediate objective revelation; or an inward voice saying, Thy sins are forgiven thee. But when the believer is examining his heart and life by the Word, the holy Spirit enlightens the mind there to discern faith, and love, and such other qualifications which the gospel declareth to be infallible signs of regeneration; and he adds such power to the testimony of conscience, for the truth and in-being of these graces, as begets in the soul a joyful sense of its reconciled state.[2]

Assurance was indeed an inner conviction of rightness with God, but to be real and valid it must be according to the evidence of Scripture and of conduct. This struggle against the Antinomians was the same one that engaged John Wesley later; and he might well have echoed Williams's words on his opponents, 'With these we are legal preachers, if we urge faith and repentance in order to pardon, though we declare that faith and repentance are the gifts of Christ.'[3]

Of these Puritan authors, Richard Baxter comes nearest to relating the doctrine of assurance to his own Christian life. For Susanna's father, however, assurance of a quiet and unspectacular kind was quite central to his experience for much of his adult life. Daniel Williams's funeral sermon for Annesley recalled that

He had uninterrupted peace and assurance of God's covenant-love for above 30 years last past. It's true, he walked in darkness for several years before that, which is common to those who are converted in childhood, their change not being remarkable, and

---

[1] D. Williams, *Gospel-Truth Stated and Vindicated* (1692), p. 161. This work was published by Annesley's son-in-law, John Dunton, and contains a commendatory preface signed by a number of ministers who were friends and fellow-workers of Annesley, including William Bates, Vincent Alsop, Richard Mayo, Richard Stretton, John Howe, and Thomas Kentish.

[2] Williams, *Gospel-Truth*, p. 160.

[3] Ibid., p. 249.

so apter to be questioned; and they oft make up, in a long time, by frequent returns, the sad hours that others have pressing in at once. But God had a further design, viz. the fitting and inclining him to relieve wounded consciences by his ministry and discourse, wherein he was so eminent, that most troubled souls resorted to him. He used to say, that this made him unable to preach a sermon without some word to them.[1]

We have confirmation of Williams's account from Susanna herself. On Monday, 3rd September 1739, shortly after a turning-point in her own spiritual life, she was discussing with John the subject of assurance of the forgiveness of sins. She confessed that, until two or three weeks before, she had been a stranger both to the doctrine and the experience. John then asked her 'whether her father had not the same faith; and whether she had not heard him preach it to others. She answered he had it himself; and declared, a little before his death, that for more than forty years he had no darkness, no fear, no doubt at all of his being 'accepted in the Beloved'. But that, nevertheless, she did not remember to have heard him preach—no, not once—explicitly upon it; whence she supposed he also looked upon it as the peculiar blessing of a few, not as promised to all the people of God'.[2] This account is consistent both with her father's published sermons, which do not treat explicitly of this matter, and with Williams's account of his intense pastoral concern for 'troubled souls'. It seems likely that he would not publicize his own experience of confident assurance, lest those not granted it should be discouraged, or think it an indispensable token of the true believer. Further corroboration of Dr Annesley's experience comes from his daughter Elizabeth, who after her father's death, exclaimed, 'Oh what a comfort is it to us that he enjoyed such an uninterrupted assurance of heaven, and that

[1] Williams, *The Excellency of a Publick Spirit*, p. 145. The pastoral concern of Annesley for 'wounded consciences' is typical of the best Puritan preachers, for whom *Theology and the Cure of Souls*—to use the title of Dr Frederic Greeves's suggestive study—were intimately related.

[2] Wesley, *Journal*, II, 267f.

resignation of himself to the divine will, which is enough to make all that have been about him in love with the ways of God, and may afford us comfort under our great loss.'[1]

This aspect of Puritan teaching seems by her own account to have been lost on Susanna; yet the outstanding example of her father's assurance must have formed a constant element in her spiritual background. John's questioning of his mother as to 'whether her father had not the same faith', suggests that he too knew something of his grandfather's experience, or that he assumed such teaching to be integral to the Puritan tradition in which Annesley stood.[2] Of course, Wesley would have gone further than Annesley in his statement of the doctrine, for he emphatically believed, at this time, that a personal assurance of forgiveness was 'promised to all the people of God',—though he modified this view in later life. To transpose Doolittle's metaphor, Wesley held that this grace of assurance was intended to serve Christians, not 'for a spiritual banquet', 'but 'for a standing-dish'. At this point Susanna's Puritanism seems to have become somewhat diluted. In becoming a Methodist, she was to make a break-through to assurance, and to recapture the sort of joy in the Christian life which her father had known.

Wesley's *Journal* contains a memorable account of what happened to his mother. On Monday, 3rd September 1739, he recorded:

I talked largely with my mother, who told me that, till a short time since, she had scarce heard such a thing mentioned as the having forgiveness of sins now, or God's Spirit bearing witness with our spirit; much less did she imagine that this was the common privilege of all true believers. 'Therefore,' said she, 'I never durst ask for it myself. But two or three weeks ago, while my son Hall was pronouncing those words, in delivering the cup to me, "The blood of our Lord Jesus Christ, which was

[1] Rogers, *Character of a Good Woman*, p. 166.
[2] John and his mother had discussed assurance by letter as early as 1725. See Wesley, *Works*, XII, 8f., and J. S. Simon, *John Wesley and the Religious Societies* (1921), p. 81f.

given for thee," the words struck through my heart, and I knew God for Christ's sake had forgiven *me* all *my* sins'.[1]

When three years later Charles Wesley composed his mother's epitaph, he enshrined this moment in some lines which might well have been taken from one of his 'Hymns on the Lord's Supper':

> The Father then revealed His Son,
> Him in the broken bread made known;
> She knew and felt her sins forgiven,
> And found the earnest of her heaven.

Being Charles, however, and the son of his father, his innate tendency to extremism would not allow him to stop there. He must go on to write a couplet which blandly dismissed his mother's seventy years of life as lived under the law, not under grace. With a quite grotesque bigotry, he described her as having 'mourned a long night of grief and fears, a legal night of seventy years'! This view may have accorded well with Charles's rigid and at times rather inhuman scheme of salvation, but it did scant justice to the fact that it was in this 'legal night' that he had himself first seen the light of the gospel, and been grounded by his mother in Christian truth and love.

If we reject Charles's version of this phase of his mother's spiritual life, how are we to interpret it? It would seem that here she had lost, or grown away from, her Puritan heritage in a measure, though Dr Annesley's reticence on the subject should be noted. Yet the doctrine and experience of assurance were certainly known among the Puritans, and her father's colleague, Thomas Doolittle, in one of his sermons strikingly anticipates Susanna's experience at the sacrament. He pointed to Holy Communion as a divinely-appointed means by which believers might receive assurance of their pardon, and asked each member of the congregation:

---

[1] Wesley, *Journal*, II, 267. Her 'son Hall' was Westley Hall, an Anglican clergyman married to her daughter, Martha.

Art thou not too much guilty of hypocrisy, when thou goest to the table of the Lord, and yet dost not give diligence to make thy calling and election sure; nor to have the certain knowledge of the pardon of thy sin, and of thy peace with God? Is not the Lord's supper an ordinance for the helping the right receivers to assurance of the pardon of their sin, in the blood of Christ? Is it not for that end a seal of the covenant of grace? If thou sayest thou usest it for this end, why then dost thou look after it no more, when thou returnest from that ordinance?[1]

If, then, we cannot accept Charles's over-dramatized and uncharitable view of his mother's experience at the sacrament, we must still grant that 1739 did mark a real turning-point in her spiritual life. It is perhaps significant that her experience, like her father's, was described in terms of *illumination*. Once assured of his acceptance with God, Dr Annesley had 'no more darkness' afterwards; and though Susanna's previous life had certainly not been spent in 'legal night', she did after 1739 apprehend more plainly and perfectly Him in whom there is no darkness at all. It cannot be contended that Susanna knew nothing of the forgiveness of God before that date, but thereafter she knew it with a new depth of personal awareness and certainty. It was as though an element in her spiritual heritage which had been dormant, awakened suddenly into vibrant life. The teaching of the Puritan divines who made up her father's circle, Dr Annesley's known experience of assurance, and her own half-realized grasp of the doctrine,[2] all coalesced in her new awareness of forgiveness. At this late stage of her pilgrimage, Susanna may be said to have reversed the order of historical development from Puritanism to the Age of Reason, and to have entered more fully into the living tradition of her Puritan forbears.

[1] *The Morning-Exercise at Cripplegate*, ed. Annesley, p. 316 (2).

[2] As Adam Clarke, *Wesley Family*, II, 73, points out, Susanna, expounding 'I believe in the Holy Ghost', 'hints at that doctrine . . . which is a standard article in the creed of every Methodist, viz., *The doctrine of the witness of the Spirit in the souls of genuine believers*. Her words are strong and pointed : "It is he that leadeth us into all truth. He helpeth our infirmities, assures us of our adoption, and will be with the Holy Catholic Church to the end of the world!" '

Certainly it was the Methodist preaching of assurance—that a believer could know his sins forgiven in this life—which above all touched the eighteenth century exponents of reasonable religion on the raw. Here, we may venture to say, the seventeenth century triumphed over the eighteenth in Susanna, and the Puritanism in which she was bred found a new force and vigour when she cast in her spiritual lot with the Methodists.

CHAPTER EIGHT

Holy Dying

Christian, make it the study and business of thy life to
learn to do thy last work well.   *Richard Baxter*
When we see the day approaching, we must address
ourselves to our dying work with all seriousness,
renewing our repentance for sin, our consent to the
covenant, our farewells to the world; and our souls
must be carried out towards God in suitable breathings.
Matthew Henry

T H E Puritan would have been appalled at the
modern tendency to surround a dying man with a conspiracy
of silence, until, drugged and insensible, he is able to shuffle
off this mortal coil without ever really facing death. If for
the Puritan life was real, life was earnest, then so was death.
As he addressed himself to his 'dying work', he maintained
his attitude of high seriousness to the end. His response to
dying, as to everything else in life, was active and positive.
For him, it was the final deed to be done, the ultimate
battle to be fought, and in this strenuous spirit he squared up
to the last enemy.

Death was for the Puritan, however, more than a personal

test, the final conflict of the life of faith. It was also an opportunity to give glory to God and to build up others in the faith. The enormous literature of Puritan funeral sermons makes clear the edification to be drawn from a believer's death-bed, either by those who witnessed his end, or by those who heard or read of it later. No doubt some of these sermons tend to idealize, to soften the harsh reality of a painful illness or a dying agony. Yet in some of the greatest descriptions of Puritan death-bed scenes, it is the verisimilitude that commands respect. Baxter could expatiate on 'the great difference between the death of a heavenly believer and of an earthly sensualist', and extol the former as 'a comfortable death'. But by 'comfortable' he did not mean a death void of physical pain, as the context of the phrase and the manner of his own dying both make plain. 'It wonderfully prepareth for a comfortable death', he writes, 'to live in the fellowship of the sufferings of Christ;'[1] and the day before he died he said to his friends, with the honesty that was ingrained in him, 'I have pain, there is no arguing against sense, but I have peace, I have peace.'[2]

It was in this great Puritan tradition of holy dying that Susanna was found as she took her leave of the world. It was a tradition which her own father had adorned with his last words of triumphant faith: 'I'll die praising thee, and rejoice that there's others can praise thee better. I shall be satisfied with thy likeness; satisfied, satisfied! Oh my dearest Jesus I come.'[3] The same longing to give glory to God *in articulo mortis* breaks out again in John Wesley's dying words, 'I'll praise, I'll praise . . .' With unconscious aptness, Wesley's lips take up the words of one of the greatest hymns of the Puritan tradition, Isaac Watts's 'I'll praise my Maker'. No words could better express the strength and confidence of the

---

[1] Baxter, *Practical Works*, ed. Orme XVIII, 7–8.
[2] Baxter, *Autobiography*, ed. Lloyd Thomas, p. 266.
[3] Williams, *The Excellency of a Publick Spirit*, p. 146.

Godward reference of Puritan faith than these; the resolve that, to the very last breath, life is to be expended *ad maiorem Dei gloriam*:

> I'll praise my Maker, while I've breath;
> And when my voice is lost in death,
> Praise shall employ my nobler powers;
> My days of praise shall ne'er be past,
> While life, and thought, and being last,
> Or immortality endures.

So at the very end Wesley joins himself to the Puritan succession of faith, and echoes, in a strangely moving way, his grandfather's words of nearly a century before, 'I'll die praising thee.'

Fifteen years before Susanna died, she and John had discussed in their letters the time when death must part them. John expressed a wish to die before his mother—scarcely a natural desire in a young man of twenty-four, but one which suggests the powerful ties which bound Wesley to his mother. She replied with her usual sobriety and common sense:

You did well to correct that fond desire of dying before me, since you do not know what work God may have for you to do ere you leave the world. And besides, I ought surely to have the pre-eminence in point of time, and go to rest before you. Whether you could see me die without any emotions of grief, I know not; perhaps you could; it is what I have often desired of the children, that they would not weep at our parting, and so make death more uncomfortable than it would otherwise be to me. If you, or any other of my children, were like to reap any spiritual advantage by being with me at my exit, I should be glad to have you with me. But as I have been an unprofitable servant, during the course of a long life, I have no reason to hope for so great an honour, so high a favour, as to be employed in doing our Lord any service in the article of death. It were well if you spake prophetically, and that joy and hope might have the ascendant over the other passions of my soul in that important hour. Yet I dare not presume, nor do I despair, but rather leave it to our Almighty Saviour, to do with me both in life and death just what he pleases, for I have no choice.[1]

[1] Clarke, *Wesley Family*, II, 26–7. Letter dated 26 July 1727.

The fact that Susanna had often spoken to her children about her death suggests a certain degree of preparedness for it, however diffident she might feel about her own adequacy for 'that important hour'. Her hope that her children might be edified by her departing, her desire to serve Christ even in the act of dying, and her utter resignation to the divine will, —these show the lasting influence upon her soul of the Puritan piety in which she had been formed. There are, nevertheless, hints in the letter of a certain uneasiness in face of death, which she expects to be harrowing experience even if her children's grief does not make it more so. This suggestion of unreadiness, of shrinking back from the moment of death, is touched on in a letter to John written eight years later. She acknowledges, with typical candour, that, though she has long since chosen God as her 'only God' and her 'All', yet 'one thing often troubles me, that, notwithstanding I know that while we are present with the body we are absent from the Lord; notwithstanding I have no taste, no relish left for anything the world calls pleasure, yet I do not long to go home as in reason I ought to do. This often shocks me: and as I constantly pray (almost without ceasing) for thee, my son; so I beg you likewise to pray for me, that God would make me better, and take me at the best.'[1]

For all her forebodings, however, the experience of death, when it came to her in the summer of 1742, found Susanna calm and well-prepared. At the end of July, John Wesley rode from Bristol to London, and recorded in his *Journal*, 'I found my mother on the borders of eternity. But she had no doubt or fear; nor any desire but (as soon as God should call) "to depart, and to be with Christ".' The calm and peace of her passing are described more fully in John's entry for 30th July, the day on which Susanna died.[2] 'About three in the afternoon,' he records:

[1] Clarke, *Wesley Family*, II, 31–2.

[2] The *Journal* (III, 29) has 23 July, but Wesley's letters make plain that the date was in fact 31 July 1742.

I went to my mother, and found her change was near. I sat
down on the bed-side. She was in her last conflict; unable to
speak, but, I believe, quite sensible. Her look was calm and
serene, and her eyes fixed upward, while we commended her soul
to God. From three to four the silver cord was loosing and the
wheel breaking at the cistern; and then, without any struggle, or
sigh, or groan, the soul was set at liberty. We stood round her
bed, and fulfilled her last request, uttered a little before she lost
her speech: 'Children, as soon as I am released, sing a psalm of
praise to God.'[1]

Her daughter Anne's account in a letter to Charles is similar
and equally circumstantial:

A few days before my mother died, she desired me, if I had
strength to bear it, that I would not leave her till death, which
God enabled me to do. She laboured under great trials both of
soul and body, some days after you left her; but God perfected
His work in her about twelve hours before He took her to Himself. She waked out of a slumber; and we, hearing her rejoicing,
attended to the words she spoke, which were these: 'My dear
Saviour! are you come to help me in my extremity at last?'
From that time she was sweetly resigned indeed; the enemy had
no more power to hurt her. The remainder of her time was
spent in praise.[2]

If ever a mother deserved to die with her children round
her, it was Susanna. They were not all there, of course, for
Samuel was dead before her, and Charles out of London;
but John was present, together with 'three or four of our
sisters', as he wrote to his brother. She was still their teacher
and instructress in the faith, as she pledged them to 'sing a
psalm of praise to God', as they had done at her instance
innumerable times in their Epworth days. She proved their
exemplar in dying, as she had been in living, and John's
observation on the members of his societies, 'Our people die
well,' proves his mother, once more, a true Methodist.

Yet though a Methodist now, Susanna remained an
Anglican too, and the Prayer Book found its fitting place in

[1] Wesley, *Journal*, III, 29–30.
[2] Stevenson, *Memorials of the Wesley Family*, pp. 225–6.

her dying moments. In his letter to Charles, John included a detail which is absent from the account in his *Journal*: 'After using the Commendatory prayer, I sat down on her bedside, and, with three or four of our sisters, sang a requiem to her departing soul.'[1] John here presumably refers to the familiar prayer in the 'Order for the Visitation of the Sick', which the 1662 Prayer Book entitled 'A commendatory Prayer for a sick person at the point of departure'. It commended Susanna, as she had often commended herself, 'into the hands of a faithful Creator, and most merciful Saviour'. It besought that her soul might be purged from 'whatsoever defilements it may have contracted in the midst of this miserable and naughty world',—and both adjectives should be given due weight, to do justice to Susanna's experience of the human condition. It closed with the petition, 'And teach us who survive, in this and other like daily spectacles of mortality, to see how frail and uncertain our own condition is: and so to number our days, that we may seriously apply our hearts to that holy and heavenly wisdom, whilst we live here, which may in the end bring us to life everlasting, through the merits of Jesus Christ thine only Son our Lord.' For those who survived this death-bed scene, there could be, in the deepest sense, no 'other like daily spectacles of mortality', for to them her death was *sui generis*, like no other. And they did not need to be present at her dying to learn the lesson that they should apply their hearts to 'that holy and heavenly wisdom', for her whole life had bidden them do nothing else.

The wheel had come full circle for Susanna. She died in London, where she was born and lived all her early life. She was buried—and none more fittingly—in what John Kirk is pleased to call 'that great Puritan Necropolis', Bunhill Fields. Her body lies among the Puritan saints, with John Bunyan, John Owen, Isaac Watts, and her own sister,

[1] See Wesley, *Journal*, III, 30n.

Elizabeth Dunton. John buried her there, on Sunday afternoon, 1st August, and preached to a great crowd at her
graveside: 'Almost an innumerable company of people being
gathered together, about five in the afternoon I committed
to the earth the body of my mother, to sleep with her fathers.'
He preached from *The Revelation*, of the great white throne
and the judgement of the dead, in the hearing of 'one of the
most solemn assemblies I ever saw, or expect to see on this
side eternity'.[1] The plain headstone which her family placed
above her grave bore some trite and undistinguished verses
by Charles, but in his closing couplets he spoke no more
than the truth:

> Meet for the fellowship above,
> She heard the call, 'Arise, My love!'
> 'I come!' her dying look replied,
> And lamb-like as her Lord, she died.

For all the constriction of her earthly circumstances, there
is a universal quality about Susanna Wesley's life and faith.
She was indeed the daughter of Puritanism, and in a real
sense the mother of Methodism. She stands as a living
embodiment of that continuity between these two move-
ments which has perhaps never been adequately recognized.
Yet above and beyond her place in a particular stream of the
Protestant tradition, she stands forth as one of the saints of
the Holy Catholic Church, with the authentic marks of
spiritual greatness upon her.

---

[1] Wesley, *Journal*, III, 30–1.

CHAPTER NINE

New Light on Susanna Wesley: 1969–2002

IN the thirty-four years since *Susanna Wesley and the Puritan Tradition in Methodism* was published, there have been significant developments both in Wesley Studies and in the role of women in Church and society. In the field of Wesley Studies, scholars have shed new light on key members of the Wesley family, both through biographical studies and through a more extensive publication of their own writings. Notable among biographies has been Dr Henry D. Rack's magisterial study, *Reasonable Enthusiast: John Wesley and the Rise of Methodism.*[1] In terms of primary source material, pride of place must be given to the *Bicentennial Edition of the Works of John Wesley* (1975–), which is still in process of publication and, when complete, will be unrivalled in its comprehensiveness and critical scholarship. It will ultimately include, 'all Wesley's original or mainly original prose works, together with one volume devoted to his *Collection of Hymns* (1780) and another to his extensive work as editor and publisher of extracts from the writings of others'.[2]

If John Wesley's writings are in process of being made fully available, the same is true of those of Charles, who has not

[1] Published 1989 by Epworth Press; 3rd edition 2002.
[2] *The Bicentennial Edition of the Works of John Wesley* (1975–), Vol. 22, Introduction, p. v. (Hereafter cited as 'BE. Wesley, *Works*').

hitherto received nearly as much scholarly attention as his older brother. Here much pioneering work has been carried out by Professor Kenneth G.C. Newport, as the Director of the Charles Wesley Research Centre at Hope University College, Liverpool. Dr Newport has already published a volume of *The Sermons of Charles Wesley*,[1] and he is now preparing a two-volume edition of Charles's Letters. In addition, he is engaged in editing the first full-length, critical edition of Charles's Journal. This major work will run to many volumes and will include a translation of all the sensitive passages which Charles recorded in shorthand, which often relate to the differences in churchmanship between John and himself. Charles once summed up the essential variance between John and himself in the following trenchant judgement: 'All the difference between my brother and me was that my brother's first object was the Methodists and then the Church; mine was first the Church and then the Methodists.'[2] Charles was indeed much more the stiff High churchman than John. In this regard, as in others, Charles resembled his father, Samuel. John, on the other hand, though a loyal churchman, was much more flexible with regard to canon law and church order. Here, he was very much his mother's son and may be seen as reverting, albeit unconsciously, to his Puritan, Nonconformist ancestry. Susanna, as we have seen, was prepared to hold unauthorized services in the rectory during her husband's enforced absence at Convocation, and, once she had become a Methodist, helped persuade John to accept a wider ministry of lay preaching within the movement.[3]

When Professor Newport's comprehensive editions of Charles's writings are complete, they will furnish materials for a fuller and more nuanced account of the rise and progress of the Methodist movement. Hitherto, the story has been written very

[1] Kenneth G.C. Newport, ed., *The Sermons of Charles Wesley*. A Critical Edition with Introduction (Oxford University Press, 2001).
[2] John Telford, ed., *The Letters of the Rev. John Wesley M.A.* (1931), 8 vols., VIII.267.
[3] See above, p. 181 for the case of Thomas Maxfield.

much from the perspective of John Wesley, as the movement's leader. The importance of Charles as hymn-writer has been amply acknowledged but in other respects his voice has been only partially heard. Recent scholarship and work now in progress should remedy that deficiency and allow the silence to be broken.

There has been similar progress in providing opportunity for Susanna to speak more adequately for herself. Here Professor Charles Wallace has produced an invaluable tool in his *Susanna Wesley: The Complete Writings*.[1] His work on Susanna was, by his own account, '. . . prompted by a concern to recover the works of women in various religious traditions . . . in their struggles and triumphs in more restrictive times and places'.[2] This wider concern to publish women's writings from previous centuries is one that has grown considerably in the last three decades. It is significant that Oxford University Press, the publishers of Susanna's *Complete Writings*, remind readers that they have also made available writings of women as diverse as Anne Askew, Hildegard of Bingen, and Lady Eleanor Davies. Yet within this wider framework of classic women's writings, Professor Wallace, as a Methodist historian, has a special interest in Susanna.

He is, of course, interested in highlighting her formative influence—direct and indirect—on the beginnings of Methodism. More than that, however, he is intent on enabling her own distinctive voice to be more fully heard, and her many-sided personality to be adequately appreciated. As he states in his Introduction,

In putting together material for this collection, I am assuming that Susanna Wesley's own writings allow her finally to speak for herself and yield a richer and fuller identity than she has ever been accorded before.[3]

---

[1] *Susanna Wesley: The Complete Writings*, ed. Charles Wallace Jr. Oxford University Press 1997. (Hereafter cited as 'Wallace').

[2] Wallace, p. 4.

[3] Ibid., *loc. cit.*

He infers that, 'Our age may not regard her as St Susanna, mother of St John, any longer, but it might justly discover her to be a competent, practical theologian-educator and a complex and extraordinary woman in her own historical context.'[1]

The *Complete Writings* comprise Susanna's Letters, Journals, and what Charles Wallace terms her 'Educational, Catechetical, and Controversial Writings'. The seventy-two Letters date from 1702 to 1741, and include thirty-six to John Wesley, which, 'focus intensely on issues of "practical divinity", imparting theological advice appropriate for the various early career changes he was going through'.[2] Professor Wallace has been able to draw on sources which were not available when I wrote in 1968, notably the Methodist Archives in the John Rylands Library of the University of Manchester. These Archives contain an important letter-book of John Wesley, in which he copied letters written to him by members of his family, including some significant ones from Susanna.

For example, on 19th August 1724, Susanna wrote to son John—still addressing him as 'Jacky', though he by this time a twenty-one-year-old Oxford graduate—a letter which breathes maternal concern, and is also typically haunted by money worries. She writes:

Dear Jacky,
 I am somewhat uneasy, because I've not heard from you so long and think you don't do well to stand upon points and write only letter for letter, since I decline apace, and 'tis more trouble for me to write one than for you to write ten times. Therefore let me hear from you oftener, and inform me of the state of your health, how you go on, and whether you are easier than formerly, and have any reasonable hopes of being out of debt.

Debt was an all too familiar fact of life in Epworth Rectory, and Susanna is anxious that John should have had to resort to borrowing money. She is also embarrassed that, in her present state, she is unable to help him repay his debts. She continues:

[1] Wallace, p. 18.
[2] Wallace, p. 31.

We have dismal weather, and can neither get hay, corn, nor firing, which makes us apprehensive of great want. I am most concerned for that good generous man that lent you £10 and am ashamed to beg a month or two longer, since he was so kind to grant us so much time already. Give my service to him and thanks, however.

She concludes, despite her continuing anxieties, with words of encouragement to John, who, like herself, must continue to contend with pressing financial worries:

Dear Jacky, be not discouraged; do your duty, keep close to your studies, and hope for better days; perhaps, notwithstanding all, we shall pick up a few crumbs for you before the end of the year.
Dear Son, I beseech Almighty God to bless thee![1]

These letters from Susanna to John serve to underline the intimate relationship between mother and son. From his birth he had held a special place in her affections, in that he was born of the reconciliation of his parents after their celebrated quarrel over the legitimacy of King William III. The rift had led Samuel to suspend marital relations with Susanna ('Madam, if we are to have two kings, we must have two beds!'), and these were only resumed after the quarrel had been resolved. Jacky was the first child born of their reunion, the seal of their reconciliation. In addition to the special circumstances of his birth, Jacky's place in his mother's affections was further reinforced by his narrow escape, as a child of six, from the fire which destroyed the rectory. Following his deliverance, Susanna took a solemn vow before God that she would, 'be more particularly careful of the soul of this child that Thou hast so mercifully provided for, than ever I have been . . .'[2] She was as good as her word, and the bond between them was accordingly further deepened.

That John Wesley reciprocated his mother's special feelings for him may be inferred from his seeking advice from her well into his adult life. Henry Rack has helpfully drawn attention, in

[1] Wallace, pp. 103–4. This letter is also printed in BE. Wesley, *Works*, Vol. 25, Letters I, 1721–1739, ed. Frank Baker (1980), p. 148.
[2] See above, p. 112.

this connexion, to Wesley's remarkable sermon, 'On Obedience to Parents', which he printed in the *Arminian Magazine* of 1784. Wesley takes the biblical injunction to 'Honour thy father and mother' to entail lifelong obedience to parents, and confesses.

When I had lived upwards of thirty years I looked upon myself to stand just in the same relation to my father as I did when I was ten years old. And when I was between forty and fifty I judged myself as much obliged to obey my mother in everything lawful as I did when I was in my hanging-sleeve coat.[1]

Wesley's strict interpretation of the injunction to obey parents needs, as Rack points out, to be tested against his actual behaviour when it came to a difference of judgement between him and one of his parents. He was not prepared, for example, to accept his father's strong request, in 1734, that he should leave Oxford and return to Lincolnshire to succeed his ageing parent as Rector of Epworth. Again, when it came to his mother's will for him, his obedience was by no means unconditional. He drew the line at the crucial point of deciding on a marriage partner. In 1781, in a revealing letter to Elijah Bush, one of his itinerant preachers, he urged Bush never to marry without his parents' consent to his choice of wife:

I was much concerned yesterday when I heard you were likely to marry a woman against the consent of your parents. I have never in an observation of fifty years known such a marriage attended with a blessing. I know not how it should be, since it is flatly contrary to the fifth commandment. I told my own mother, when pressing me to marry, 'I dare not allow you a positive voice herein; I dare not marry a person because you bid me. But I must allow you a negative voice: I will marry no person if you forbid. I know it would be a sin against God.' Take care what you do.[2]

It is not known whether Susanna ever exercised any formal veto on a possible marriage partner for her son. What is clear,

---

[1] BE. Wesley, *Works*, Vol. 3, Sermons III, 71–114, ed. Albert C. Outler (1986), p. 364. See also Rack, *Reasonable Enthusiast*, p. 56.

[2] See Bufford W. Coe, *John Wesley and Marriage* (London: Associated University Presses, 1996), p. 81, citing *The Letters of the Rev. John Wesley, A.M.*, ed. J. Telford, 8 vols., 1931, 7: 83–4.

from John's own account, is the overwhelming influence of Susanna on his ideal of womanhood and on his model of what a wife should be. In his private diary, he records his thoughts on celibacy and marriage, and gives a number of reasons, both practical and theological, for his conviction that he is called to the single life. Significantly, the reason he places first in the list goes back to his childhood and to the potent influence of Susanna:

1. From the time I was Six or Seven years old, if any one spoke to me concerning marrying, I used to say, I thought I never should, 'Because I should never find such a woman as my Father had.'

The other reasons he gives are a mixture of the practical and the theological:

2. When I was about Seventeen (and so till I was Six or Seven and twenty) I had no thought of marrying, 'Because I could not keep a Wife.'
3. I was then persuaded, 'It was unlawful for a Priest to marry,' grounding that Persuasion on the (supposed) Sense of the Primitive Church.
4. Not long after, by reading some of the Mystic Writers, I was brought to think 'Marriage was the less Perfect state,' and that there was some degree (at least) of 'Taint upon the Mind, necessarily attending the Marriage-Bed.'
5. At the same time I view'd in a strong light St Paul's words to the Corinthians: And judg'd it 'impossible for a married man to be so without carefulness, or to attend upon the Lord with so little Distraction, as a single man might do.'
6. Likewise, being desirous to lay out all I could in feeding the hungry and cloating [sic] the naked, I could not think of marrying, 'because it would bring such Expense, as would swallow up all I now give away.'
7. But my grand Objection for these twelve years past has been, 'A Dispensation of the Gospel has been committed to me. And I will do nothing which directly or indirectly tends to hinder my preaching the Gospel.'[1]

There is no need to doubt Wesley's sincerity in citing such prudential, practical, and religious reasons for remaining a celibate. Yet it is hard to resist the conclusion that these later

[1] Cited in Coe, *John Wesley and Marriage*, p. 58.

reasons are subordinate to the first one he adduces, going back to his early years, his conviction that he, 'should never find such a woman as my Father had'.

I have written elsewhere, in a brief study of 'Wesley and Women', of the,

> . . . particularly close bond between mother and son, which endured to her death and no doubt beyond. That is not to imply that the umbilical cord was never cut, or that Wesley was held in infantile dependence on his mother. He grew up, as did his brothers and sisters, into a spirited independence of character. Yet the bond, even in his maturity, still held.[1]

John Wesley had numerous women friends, correspondents, helpers, whom in his letters he characteristically addresses as, 'My dear Sister . . .' Yet it remains true that, 'Susanna had set the standard of womanhood for him. It was a high standard, so high, perhaps, that no other woman could ever attain to it. John Wesley gave and received much in his wide range of friendships with women; they were to him advisers, co-adjutors, supporters, and colleagues. His mother had been to him all these and more. Though he might have many "Sisters", he had only one mother. He remained, first and last, "Son to Susanna"'.[2]

Dr Bufford W. Coe's recent study of *John Wesley and Marriage* (1996), which I have drawn on here, has served to underline Susanna's crucial relationship with her son, and its influence on John's attitudes to other women. There have been a number of other areas, over the last three decades, in which our understanding of Susanna and her world has been considerably enhanced. More light has been shed on her own upbringing, as the daughter of Dr Samuel Annesley, the distinguished Puritan pastor and theologian. Mrs Betty Young, a Librarian at Duke University, North Carolina, has carried out detailed research,

[1] J.A. Newton, 'Wesley and Women', in *John Wesley: Contemporary Perspectives*, ed. John Stacey (Epworth Press, 1988), p. 133.
[2] Ibid., p. 137.

using seventeenth-century parish registers, wills, and correspondence, to explore Susanna's family background, in her
article 'Sources for the Annesley Family'.[1] In particular, she
draws attention to Mary Annesley, Susanna's mother, who, as
she rightly infers, 'must have been a remarkable woman'.
Citing Roger Thompson's *Women in Stuart England and America*
(1974), which concludes that in the seventeenth century girls
usually received their education from their mothers, Mrs
Young ventures the judgement that, 'Susanna, as one of the
Annesley children, must have brought the training of her
mother, as well as that of "Dr Annesley", to her influence on
her sons. Like her mother she had to cope with the responsibility of rearing a large number of children with a husband who
was sometimes absent and always busy. Perhaps Susanna's
well-known methodical approach to the task was copied from
her own childhood upbringing'.[2]

The same number of the *Proceedings of the Wesley Historical
Society* (September 1985), which carried Mrs Young's essay, also
contained an article which I devoted to 'Samuel Annesley
(1620–1696)'.[3] It examines the life and ministry of this distinguished representative of seventeenth-century Nonconformity.
It explores the close relationship between Annesley and
Susanna, his favourite daughter. It also examines how far
Annesley's impact on John Wesley may be seen as an aspect of
that Puritan–Methodist continuity for which I have argued
elsewhere.[4] As far as Susanna is concerned, I sought to show
that,

Loyalty to conscience, humility before God and boldness in the face of
men, and a zeal for practical godliness: these were the traits which Dr
Annesley shared with his daughter. She, in turn, by teaching and

[1] Betty Irene Young, 'Sources for the Annesley Family', *Proceedings of the Wesley
Historical Society* (Hereafter 'PWHS'), Vol. XLV.Pt.2, September 1985, pp. 44–57.
[2] Ibid., p. 57.
[3] John A. Newton, 'Samuel Annesley (1620–1696)', PWHS, Vol. XLV.Pt.2,
September 1985, pp. 29–45.
[4] J.A. Newton, 'Methodism and the Puritans', Friends of Dr Williams's Library
Lecture, 1964.

example, inculcated these same virtues in the minds of her children, including, most notably, John Wesley himself.[1]

Another development which has enabled a fuller under-standing of Susanna's life and work has been the proliferation of women's studies which help place her against the back-ground of her culture. These studies include Sheila Row-botham's *Hidden from History: Rediscovering Women in History from the 17th Century to the Present* (1974); Mary Prior, ed., *Women in English Society, 1500–1800* (1985); and Patricia Crawford's *Women and Religion in England 1500–1720* (1993). My own biography con-sidered Susanna primarily in relation to Methodism, with due regard to her Puritan formation and her leaving Non-conformity for the Church of England. These more general studies of the life of women in seventeenth and eighteenth-century England allow us to set her in a wider context, rather than seeing her simply as 'Mother of the Wesleys' or as the 'Mother of Methodism'.

Finally, the growing interest in women's writing in theology and spirituality has led to a number of illuminating studies of Susanna's teaching and religious experience. Future explo-ration in this field will be much indebted to Charles Wallace's pioneering work in publishing—in *Susanna Wesley: The Complete Writings*—the first comprehensive, critical edition of her de-votional journals and theological writings. He points out that, '. . . diaries were, in addition to letters, the main mode of written self-expression open to early eighteenth-century women.'[2] Here again, recent scholarship has provided much illuminating background to Susanna's diary-keeping. Two works singled out by Wallace are: Sara Heller Mendelson's 'Stuart Women's Diaries and Occasional Memoirs', in Mary Prior ed., *Women in English Society 1500–1800* (1985), and Harriett Blodgett, *Centuries of Female Days: Englishwomen's Private Diaries* (1988). Professor Wallace himself places Susanna in this wider context in his

[1] Newton, PWHS, XLV.Pt.2, p. 41.
[2] Wallace, p. 198.

article, 'Susanna Wesley's Spirituality: The Freedom of a Christian Woman'.[1] He emphasizes that, 'even in the midst of the conflicting claims of wife, mother and *de facto* head of the household, she continued to pursue a contemplative vocation, the contours of which are visible to us in her devotional journal'. Hence, he argues, 'to the extent that this tension is not unique, and because she was such a remarkable and influential woman, Susanna Wesley's "inner history" may usefully serve as a case study in the history of women and religion, until lately a neglected corner of research'. He concludes that Susanna, 'as seen from the evidence of her devotional journal, represents a kind of "missing link" in the history of women and western religion. She may be seen, on the one hand, as the somewhat tamed successor of Puritan prophetesses and, on the other, as the hopeful predecessor of women fired by the eighteenth-century revival (and, paradoxically, by the ascendancy of rationalism in the same century) for non-traditional roles.'[2]

Dr Michael McMullen has made available two brief but representative selections of Susanna's devotional writings. In 1995, he published *Hearts Aflame: Prayers of Susanna, John and Charles Wesley*. He followed this in 1999 with a volume devoted solely to *Prayers and Meditations of Susanna Wesley*. Both of these handy paperbacks make Susanna's devotions easily accessible to readers who may not have access to Professor Wallace's 500-page edition of Susanna's *Complete Writings*. Dr McMullen's choice of Susanna's prayers brings out her impressive union of active service and the life of contemplation.

In sum, then, we may be grateful that we now have an unprecedented wealth of material for understanding the mind and work of an outstanding Christian woman. From her own writings, available now in their fullness, she speaks to us in her own distinctive voice. Her sons, John and Charles, are both

[1] Charles Wallace, 'Susanna Wesley's Spirituality; The Freedom of a Christian Woman', *Methodist History*, XXII:3 (1984), pp. 158–73.
[2] Wallace, pp. 159–60.

included in the Calendar of saints in the Church of England's *Alternative Service Book* of 1980. They are commemorated, appropriately enough, on the 24th of May, as 'Priests, Poets, Teachers of the Faith'. Their mother was neither priest nor poet; but she was most certainly an impressive teacher of the Faith, and without her devoted nurture her sons might well never have featured on the Calendar, nor occupied the place they have in Christian history. That is one measure—though by no means the only one—of her greatness.

BIBLIOGRAPHY

Common Abbreviations

Clarke, *Wesley Family*	Adam Clarke, *Memoirs of the Wesley Family*.
D.N.B.	*Dictionary of National Biography*.
Dunton, *Life and Errors*.	*The Life and Errors of John Dunton, Citizen of London*, ed. J. B. Nichols.
Headingley MSS A, B, C	Three duodecimo MS volumes of writings by Susanna Wesley, in the Library of Wesley College, Bristol.
Headingley MSS A	A volume inscribed inside the front cover, in Susanna's handwriting, "S.W. 1709". Ff. 62–192 contain prayers and meditations written by Susanna.
Headingley MSS B	A volume entitled "Poems &c by the Revd. Samuel Wesley, Rector of Epworth. And Meditations and Reflexions by Mrs. Susanna Wesley wife to the above."
Headingley MSS C	A volume containing: (a) a letter from Susanna to Samuel Wesley junior, dated "Epworth 11 Oct. 1709."; (b) a letter from Susanna to her daughter Sukey, expounding the Apostles' Creed, and dated "Epworth Jan.14. 1709/10."; (c) another letter from Susanna to Sukey expounding the Ten Commandments; and (d) part of Susanna's devotional journal, with meditations for morning, noon and night.
Proceedings of W.H.S.	*Proceedings of the Wesley Historical Society*.
W.H.S. Pubns.	*Publications of the Wesley Historical Society*.

ANON., *Some Remarks on a Letter from the Reverend Mr. Whitefield to the Reverend Mr. Wesley, in a Letter from a Gentlewoman to her Friend*, 1741.

A Supplement to the Morning-Exercise at Cripplegate: or, Several More Cases of Conscience Practically Resolved by Sundry Ministers, ed. Samuel Annesley, 1676.

ANNESLEY, Samuel, *A Sermon Preached to the Honourable House of Commons, July 26, 1648*, 1648.

ANNESLEY, Samuel, *A Sermon Preached at the Funeral of Reverend Mr. Will. Whitaker, Late Minister of Magdalen Bermondsey*, 1673.

ANNESLEY, Samuel, *The Life and Funeral Sermon of the Reverend Mr. Thomas Brand*, 1692.

Arminian Magazine, The, 1778–

Athenian Mercury, The, 1691–

BAKER, Frank, *Charles Wesley as Revealed by his Letters*, London, 1948.

BAKER, Frank, 'Salute to Susanna', *Methodist History*, Vol. VII, No. 3, April 1969, pp. 3–12.

BAKER, Frank, 'Susanna Wesley: Puritan, Parent, Pastor, Protagonist, Pattern', *Epworth Review*, Vol. IX, No. 2, May 1982, pp. 39–46.

BATES, William, *A Funeral-Sermon for the Reverend, Holy and Excellent Divine, Mr. Richard Baxter*, 1692.

BATHURST, Elizabeth, *An Expostulatory Appeal to the Professors of Christianity, Joyned in Community with Samuel Ansley [sic]*, n.d.

BAXTER, Richard, *The Divine Life*, 1664.

BAXTER, Richard, *A Christian Directory*, 1673.

BAXTER, Richard, *The Practical Works of the Rev. Richard Baxter*, ed. W. Orme, 23 vols., 1830.

BAXTER, Richard, *The Autobiography of Richard Baxter*, ed. J. M. Lloyd Thomas, London, n.d.

BEECHAM, H. A., 'Samuel Wesley Senior: New Biographical Evidence', *Renaissance and Modern Studies*, VII, 1963.

Bibliotheca Annesleiana: or a Catalogue of Choice Greek, Latin, and English Books, both Ancient and Modern . . . being the Library of the Reverend Samuel Annesley, L.L.D. And Minister of the Gospel Lately Deceas'd, 1697.

BRAILSFORD, Mabel R., *Susanna Wesley, the Mother of Methodism*, London, 1938.

CALAMY, Edmund, *A Continuation of the Account of the Ministers, Lecturers, Masters and Fellows of Colleges, and Schoolmasters, who were Ejected and Silenced after the Restoration in 1660, by or before the Act of Uniformity*, 2 vols., 1727.

CLARKE, Adam, *Memoirs of the Wesley Family; collected principally from original documents*, 2 vols., 1836.

CLARKE, Eliza, *Susanna Wesley*, 1876.

CRAGG, G., *Puritanism in the Period of the Great Persecution, 1660–1688*, Cambridge, 1957.

DAVIES, Horton, *The Worship of the English Puritans*, London, 1948.

DAVIES, Horton, *Worship and Theology in England from Watts and Wesley to Maurice, 1690–1850*, London, 1961.

D.F., *The Character of the late Dr. Samuel Annesley, By Way of Elegy*, 1697.

DOUGHTY, W. L., *The Prayers of Susanna Wesley*, London, 1956.

DOUGLAS, David C., *English Scholars 1660–1730*, London, 1951.

DUNTON, John, *The Life and Errors of John Dunton, Citizen of London*, ed. J. B. Nichols, 2 vols., 1818.

FIELD, Marion, *Susanna Wesley: a radical in the Rectory*, Godalming, Surrey, 1988.

GEREE, John, *The Character of an old English Puritane or Non-Conformist*, 1646.

GORDON, Alexander, *Freedom after Ejection: A Review (1690–1692) of Presbyterian and Congregational Nonconformity in England and Wales*, Manchester, 1917.

GREETHAM, Mary, *Susanna Wesley, Mother of Methodism*, Peterborough, 1988.

HALLER, William, *The Rise of Puritanism*, New York, 1938.

HARMER, Rebecca Lamar, *Susanna, Mother of the Wesleys*, London, 1968.

HARRISON, G. Elsie, *Son to Susanna: the private life of John Wesley*, London, 1937.

KIRK, John, *The Mother of the Wesleys*, 1864.

MCMULLEN, Michael D., ed., *Hearts aflame: prayers of Susanna, John and Charles Wesley*, London, 1995.

NEWTON, John A., 'Susanna Wesley (1669–1742): A bibliographical survey', *Proceedings of the Wesley Historical Society*, Vol. XXXVII, 1969–70, pp. 37–40.

NEWTON, John A., 'Samuel Annesley (1620–1696)' (The Wesley Historical Society Lecture 1985), *Proceedings of the Wesley Historical Society*, Vol. XLV, 1985–86, pp. 29–45.

ROGAL, Samuel J., 'The Epworth Woman: Susanna Wesley and her daughters', *Wesleyan Theological Journal*, Vol. 18, No. 2, Fall 1983, pp. 80–9.

ROGERS, Timothy, *The Character of a Good Woman, Both in a Single and Marry'd State*, 1697.

SCHMIDT, Martin, *John Wesley: A Theological Biography*, Vol. I, London, 1962.

STEVENSON, G. J., *Memorials of the Wesley Family*, n.d.

TALON, Henri, *John Bunyan, the man and his works*, London, 1951.

The Morning-Exercise at Cripplegate: or Several Cases of Conscience Practically

Resolved by sundry Ministers, September 1661, ed. Samuel Annesley, 1661.

TYERMAN, Luke, *The Life and Times of the Rev. Samuel Wesley, M.A.*, 1866.

WALLACE, Charles Jr., 'Susanna Wesley's spirituality: the freedom of a Christian Woman', *Methodist History*, Vol. XXII, 1983–84, pp. 158–73.

WALLACE, Charles Jr., *Susanna Wesley: The Complete Writings*, Oxford, 1997.

WEDGWOOD, Julia, *John Wesley and the Evangelical Reaction of the Eighteenth Century*, 1870.

Wesley Banner, The, 1849–52.

Wesley Historical Society Proceedings and *Publications*, 1896–.

WESLEY, John, *A Collection of Hymns for the use of the People called Methodists*, 1780.

WESLEY, John, *A Christian Library: consisting of extracts from and abridgements of the choicest pieces of Practical Divinity which have been published in the English Tongue*, ed. Thomas Jackson, 30 vols., 1819–27.

WESLEY, John, *The Works of the Rev. John Wesley, A.M.*, ed. Thomas Jackson, 14 vols., 1829–31.

WESLEY, John, *The Journal of the Rev. John Wesley, A.M.*, ed. N. Curnock, 8 vols., 1909–16.

WESLEY, John, *The Letters of the Rev. John Wesley, A.M.*, ed. J. Telford, 8 vols., 1931.

WESLEY, Samuel, *The Life of our Blessed Lord & Saviour Jesus Christ*, 1693.

WHITEFIELD, George, *Journals*, ed. I. Murray, London, 1960.

WHITING, C. E., *Studies in English Puritanism from the Restoration to the Revolution, 1660–1688*, London, 1931.

WILDER, Franklin, *Immortal Mother*, New York, 1966.

WILLIAMS, Daniel, *Gospel-Truth Stated and Vindicated*, 1692.

WILLIAMS, Daniel, *The Excellency of A Publick Spirit: Set forth in a Sermon preach'd . . . at the Funeral of that late Reverend Divine Dr. Samuel Annesley*, 1697.

YOUNG, Betty, 'Sources for the Annesley Family', *Proceedings of the Wesley Historical Society*, Vol. XLV, 1985–86, pp. 47–57.

INDEX